Friendship of My Soul

Selected Letters of Elizabeth Ann Seton
1803-1809

Compiled and Edited
by
Betty Ann McNeil, D.C.

Daughters of Charity of Saint Vincent de Paul
Emmitsburg, Maryland, USA
2010

৩৽৶

"Never let it enter your thoughts
that time, absence, or above all your carelessness in writing,
can change, even in degree a love,
a friendship of my soul
which for so many years has been as a part of itself."

Elizabeth Bayley Seton, 1810

৩৽৶

Friendship of My Soul
Selected Letters of Elizabeth Ann Seton
1803-1809

ISBN 978-0-9824936-5-6

Cover design by Stephanie Mummert. Portrait of Mrs. William Magee Seton after an engraving by Févret de Saint-Mémin for which Mrs. Seton sat in 1796. Rev. Salvator Burgio, C.M., 1950. The cameo of Saint Elizabeth Ann Seton is from the official portrait commissioned for her cause for canonization. Oil on canvas. Artist unknown, 1947.

Contents

Illustrations

Mrs. Wm. Magee Seton, Rev. Salvator Burgio, C.M., 1950,
Courtesy Daughters of Charity, Emmitsburg, Maryland.

The Widow Seton, Unidentified Artist, 1949,
Courtesy Daughters of Charity, Emmitsburg, Maryland.

Mother Seton, Attributed to Charles Bosseron Chambers, c.1931-37,
Courtesy Daughters of Charity, St. Louis, Missouri.

Preface

Friendship of My Soul presents selected letters of Elizabeth Ann Bayley Seton during a period which became pivotal for her vocation in life and journey of faith. Elizabeth Seton writes to key correspondents on matters of family, faith, and friendship. The women with whom she corresponded included a sister-in-law, the wife of her husband's business associate, and a life-long friend. Each woman shared her heart and soul with the other as they mutually supported one another during ebb and flow of the tides of their lives.

Elizabeth, Rebecca, Amabilia, and Julianna wove their lives into a rich tapestry from the warp and woof of family concerns, faith convictions, and bonds of friendship which they exchanged in correspondence when separation prevented direct conversation. The result was life-changing for Elizabeth Bayley Seton who experienced a call to religious conversion and a call to live in community and embrace a mission of service. The years Elizabeth lived in New York, Italy, and Maryland generated a Seton legacy of charity which now encircles people living in poverty around the globe.

Although Elizabeth Seton was a highly literate woman for her time, the written word in the early nineteenth century was not yet governed by the conventions of today. For the convenience of modern readers the nineteenth-century Seton texts in *Friendship of My Soul* have been edited to conform to current standards of spelling, punctuation, and grammar generally used in North America. In order for readers to gain insight into the intensity and range of feelings which Elizabeth Seton expressed in her correspondence, some words which she emphasized through capitalization have been retained.

Friendship of My Soul offers readers a glimpse into the intimate exchanges of a wife, mother, widow, and convert who became not only a spiritual leader and guide, but also a woman whose reputation for holiness continues to inspire people of faith. Today we call this humble woman Saint Elizabeth Ann Seton and ask her to intercede for God's blessings upon us and our loved ones.

Betty Ann McNeil, D.C.
Editor

Acknowledgements

Many persons have contributed to the publication of *Friendship of My Soul*, particularly a Daughter of Charity who wishes to remain anonymous but who had the vision to initiate this project and define its scope. We are grateful for her generous gift which made this publication possible. The responsibility for the accuracy of the material contained herein rests solely with me.

I would like to thank numerous individuals and institutions for their tremendous support. I am grateful for the generous enthusiasm and meticulous research and technical assistance rendered by the staff of the Daughters of Charity Archives, Emmitsburg, Maryland. No request was too demanding nor were time constraints too daunting for them whom I count among my friends and colleagues, Bonnie Weatherly, Selin James, and Mary Anne Weatherly.

I am indebted to the Sisters of Charity Federation for permission to publish documents from *Elizabeth Bayley Seton Collected Writings* and for the gracious support of Sister Judith Metz, S.C., Sister Regina Bechtle, S.C., co-editors, and Ellin M. Kelly, manuscript editor of the three volumes. They permitted the use of transcriptions and annotations as needed.

I am grateful to both Sister Judith Metz, S.C., for reviewing portions of this manuscript and Sister Joan Angermaier, D.C., for proof reading the final draft. The helpful recommendations of both were invaluable. We also appreciate the Sisters of Charity of Cincinnati, the Sisters of Charity of Saint Vincent de Paul of New York, and the Sisters of Charity of Seton Hill for permitting this project to include Seton documents to Rebecca Seton and Amabilia Filicchi. We are grateful to the Daughters of Charity Archives of both Marillac Provincialate and Saint Joseph's Provincial House for publication of artwork.

The Daughters of Charity Development and Public Relations Department has rendered timely and high-quality service in the production and design of this work. I am grateful to Lori L. Stewart, Director, for her creative insights, and to Stephanie Mummert, Graphic Designer, for her expertise and willing spirit. No request has been too minute for their consideration and timely execution.

Sister Elyse Staab, D.C., Sister Claire Debes, D.C., and their respective Provincial Councils and Sister Vincentia Goeb, D.C., Director of Heritage Ministries, made my involvement in this initiative possible and supported the hard work of transforming an idea into reality. I would like to thank the Daughters of Charity at Mother Seton House in Emmitsburg, Maryland, who provided me with a listening ear along with sisterly support and encouragement during this project.

May readers seeking to strengthen their relationship with God find a source of spiritual nourishment in Saint Elizabeth Ann Seton's experience of faith, family, and friendship presented in *Friendship of My Soul*.

Betty Ann McNeil, D.C.

Introduction
Saint Elizabeth Ann Seton (1774-1821)
Mother • Foundress • Saint

Convert to Roman Catholicism and foundress of the Sisters of Charity of St. Joseph's, the first sisterhood native to the United States, Elizabeth Bayley Seton lived her multiple vocations fully as a wife, mother, widow, sole parent, educator, social minister, and spiritual leader. Born August 28, 1774, in or near New York City, she visited Italy and also lived in Maryland, where she died at Emmitsburg, January 4, 1821. Pope Paul VI canonized her as Saint Elizabeth Ann Seton September 14, 1975. She was the first native-born resident of the United States to become a canonized saint in the Roman Catholic Church.

New York Native

The Bayley and Charlton families were among the earliest colonial settlers of the New York area. Elizabeth's paternal grandparents were William Bayley (c.1708-c.1758) and Susannah LeConte (LeCompte, b.1727), distinguished French Huguenots of New Rochelle. Her maternal grandparents, Mary Bayeux and Dr. Richard Charlton (d.1777), lived on Staten Island, where Dr. Charlton, was pastor at Saint Andrew's Episcopal Church.

Of British and French Huguenot ancestry, Elizabeth was born into a prominent Episcopalian family in New York as the second daughter of Dr. Richard Bayley (1744-1801) and Catherine Charlton (d.1777). The Bayley's first child, Mary Magdalene Bayley (1768-1856), married Dr. Wright Post (1766-1828) of New York in 1790. Catherine Bayley (1777-1778), the youngest child, died the year after the untimely death of her mother, which was probably a result of childbirth.

After the death of his first wife, Dr. Bayley wed Charlotte Amelia Barclay (1759-1805), of the Jacobus James Roosevelt lineage of New York. Their marriage, marred by marital conflict, ended in separation. The couple had seven children, three daughters and four sons. Among them was Guy Carleton Bayley (1786-1859), whose son, James Roosevelt Bayley (1814-1877), converted to Roman Catholicism and became the first bishop of Newark, New Jersey (1853-1872) and eighth archbishop of Baltimore, Maryland (1872-1877). In response to his request, Archbishop

Bayley is buried in Saint Joseph's Cemetery, the original graveyard of the Sisters of Charity at Emmitsburg, Maryland.

Elizabeth and her sister were rejected by their stepmother. On account of her father's travel abroad for medical studies, the girls lived temporarily in New Rochelle, New York, with their paternal uncle, William Bayley (1745-1811), and his wife, Sarah Pell Bayley (1741-1819). Elizabeth experienced a period of darkness about the time when her father and stepmother separated. Reflecting years later in her journal entitled *Dear Remembrances* about this period of adolescent depression, Elizabeth expressed her relief at not taking the drug laudanum, an opium derivative: "This wretched reasoning—laudanum—the praise and thanks of excessive joy not to have done the 'horrid deed'—thoughts and promise of eternal gratitude."[1]

Elizabeth had a natural bent toward contemplation. She loved nature, poetry, and music, especially the piano. Given to introspection, she frequently made entries in her journal expressing her sentiments, religious aspirations, and favorite passages from her reading of sacred scripture and literature, especially poetry.

Elizabeth met and fell in love with William Magee Seton (1768-1803), a son of William Seton, Sr. (1746-1798) and Rebecca Curzon Seton (c.1746-c.1775).[2] The couple married January 25, 1794, in the Manhattan home of Dr. Wright and Mary Bayley Post. Samuel Provoost, the first Episcopal bishop of New York, witnessed the wedding vows of the couple.

Socially Prominent

William Magee, a descendant of the Setons of Parbroath, Scotland, was the oldest of thirteen children of his father's two marriages. The elder Seton married (1767) Rebecca Curzon and the year after her death he married (1776) his sister-in-law, Anna Maria Curzon (c.1759-1792). Educated in England, William Magee, along with his father and brother James, was a founding partner in the import-export mercantile firm, the William Seton Company, which became Seton, Maitland and Company in 1793. He had visited important counting houses in Europe in 1788 and was also a friend of Filippo Filicchi (1763-1816) and Antonio Filicchi

---

[1] Regina Bechtle, S.C., and Judith Metz, S.C., eds., Ellin M. Kelly, mss. ed., *Elizabeth Bayley Seton Collected Writings*, 3 vols. (New City Press: New York, 2000-2006), 3a:513. Hereinafter cited as *Seton Collected Writings*.

[2] The name is spelled Curzon but also appears as Curson.

(1764-1847), renowned merchants of Livorno (also called Leghorn), Italy. The Filicchi family members were among his international contacts.

Socially prominent in New York, the Setons belonged to the fashionable Trinity Parish located on Broadway. Elizabeth was a devout communicant of the Episcopal Church, under the influence of Rev. John Henry Hobart (1775-1830, later bishop), who was her spiritual director. Elizabeth was among the founders and charter members of *The Society for the Relief of Poor Widows with Small Children* (1797) and also served as treasurer of the organization. Elizabeth, along with "Beck," Rebecca Mary Seton (1780-1804), her sister-in-law, soul-friend and dearest confidant, nursed the sick and dying among family, friends, and needy neighbors. When Elizabeth suspected that her sister-in-law might be lured to live in the home of her brother John Curzon Seton, she wrote Beck fondly:

> You cannot know, my Sister, the melancholy thoughts that press on me whenever I consider myself without you in Stone Street; it seems to me as if I could as soon enjoy Home without a limb or a part of myself. This no one else can understand, but I am sure you do...yet think of the children, for no one but yourself knows how necessary you are to their happiness.[3]

Wife and Mother

Happily married, Elizabeth and William Magee Seton had five children: Anna Maria (1795-1812), William (1796-1868), Richard Bayley (1798-1823), Catherine Charlton (1800-1891) and Rebecca Mary (1802-1816). Their early years of happiness, peace, and security in New York were altered forever by the terminal illness and untimely death of William Magee in Italy in 1803. The family faced prejudice, poverty, poor health, and premature deaths, not only in New York but in Maryland where they moved in 1808.

Anna Maria, who had sailed with her parents to Italy, became afflicted with tuberculosis as an adolescent but made her vows as a Sister of Charity on her deathbed. Her younger sister Rebecca fell on ice sometime before 1812, causing a hip injury which resulted in lameness and early death. Both Anna Maria and Rebecca are buried in Saint Joseph's Cemetery on the campus of the National Shrine of Saint Elizabeth Ann Seton, Emmitsburg,

[3] 1.54, Elizabeth Seton to Rebecca Seton, 10 July 1799, *Seton Collected Writings*, 1:82.

Maryland. After becoming a civil servant and sailing with the United States Navy (1822), Richard, who had nursed a victim of typhus, became infected with the disease. Richard died off the coast of Liberia on board the ship *Oswego* and was buried at sea just weeks before his 26th birthday.

Catherine Charlton (also called Josephine, her confirmation name), was beautiful and witty. She distinguished herself by her linguistic and musical talents developed at Saint Joseph's Academy, Emmitsburg. Catherine was the only Seton present at her mother's death. Catherine later lived with her brother William and his family, with whom she visited Europe several times before becoming a founding member of the Sisters of Mercy in New York City (1846). As Mother Mary Catherine, R.S.M., she devoted herself for more than forty years to prison ministry in New York.

From his youth William exhibited a passion for life at sea. He received a commission as lieutenant in the United States Navy in February of 1826. He married (1832) Emily Prime (1804-1854). Seven of their nine children lived to adulthood, including Archbishop Robert Seton (1839-1927) and Helen (1844-1906), another New York Sister of Mercy (Sister Mary Catherine, 1879-1906).

Change of Tide

After the unexpected death (1798) of her father-in-law William Seton, Sr., responsibility was thrust on Elizabeth's husband for both the Seton, Maitland and Company and the care of his younger half-siblings. About six months pregnant with her third child at the time, Elizabeth managed both families in the Seton household. There she chose to home school the youngest of her sisters-in-law and discovered enjoyment in teaching, Charlotte (1786-1853), Henrietta (Harriet) (1787-1809), and Cecilia (1791-1810). This was Elizabeth's first experience as a teacher and it became foundational for her future.

Subsequently international piracy abroad and economic factors in America arose to severely challenge the Setons' prosperity, their family business, and their security. During the ensuing financial crisis Elizabeth assisted her husband at night by doing the account books of his firm, but the company went bankrupt in 1801. The Setons lost their possessions and the family home in lower Manhattan. As their financial problems escalated William Magee began to show evidence of tuberculosis.

Faith-filled Journey

In a desperate effort to restore William Magee's health, Elizabeth and their oldest daughter, Anna Maria, accompanied him on a sea voyage to Italy. They hoped that the warm climate of Tuscany would restore his health. Italian authorities at the port of Livorno had learned that yellow fever was prevalent in New York and feared the Setons were its carriers. As a result the officials quarantined the Setons in the cold, stone San Jacopo Lazaretto. The Filicchi family did all they could to advocate for them and to provide some relief during their month of isolation but William Magee's health deteriorated beyond recovery. Two weeks after his release, William Magee died in Pisa December 27, 1803, and was buried in the English cemetery in Livorno. Elizabeth, a widow at age twenty-nine, had five young children to raise alone.

The experiences in Italy of Elizabeth and her daughter (now called Annina) transformed their lives forever. Antonio Filicchi (1764-1847) and his wife, Amabilia Baragazzi Filicchi (1773-1853) provided gracious hospitality to the widow and child until the Setons returned to the United States the next spring. Filippo and his wife, the former Mary Cowper (1760-1821) of Boston, along with Antonio and Amabilia Filicchi, introduced Elizabeth to Roman Catholicism.

In a letter to her Italian hostess Elizabeth wrote of Amabilia's "upright and happy Soul" indicating that she could "never imagine the struggles and distresses" Elizabeth had experienced since the Setons had left Livorno. "Certainly it was not easy to write to one as dear to me as you are without expressing it," Elizabeth wrote.[4] At Amabilia's home, Elizabeth came upon the text of the *Memorare*. This prayer to the Blessed Virgin prompted her to inquire about Catholic practices, first from her lack of familiarity with the religion, then from an inquisitiveness arising out of sincere interest. She asked about the Sacred Liturgy, the Real Presence in the Eucharist, and the Church's direct unbroken link with Christ and the apostles. Hers was a quest for truth. *The Italian Journal*, a long memoir written for her sister-in-law Rebecca Seton, reveals the intimate details of Elizabeth's heart-rending personal journey of inner conflict and conversion.[5] Antonio, who had business interests in America, accompanied the Setons back to America and instructed Elizabeth about the faith. He connected her with spiritual

---

[4] 3.24, Elizabeth Seton to Amabilia Filicchi, 15 April 1805, *Seton Collected Writings*, 1:353.

[5] 2.1-2.12; 2.14, Journal to Rebecca Seton, *Seton Collected Writings*, 1:243-304.

guides in the United States, including Bishop John Carroll (1735-1815, later archbishop), and also provided wise counsel during the ensuing period of agonizing indecision. Elizabeth felt deeply for Antonio, who provided not only emotional support but also substantial financial resources to help care for her family.

Although Elizabeth had left the United States a firm Protestant, she returned to New York in June of 1804 with the heart of a Roman Catholic. Opposition and insecurity immediately threatened her resolve. Elizabeth's religious inclinations incurred the ire of both family and friends. Their hostility coupled with the premature death of Rebecca Seton, her beloved sister-in-law and most intimate confidant, caused Elizabeth deep anguish. She was also troubled by her strained financial situation which made her dependent on the generosity of others. Her five children were all less than eight years of age. As their sole parent Elizabeth dealt with much stress and faced many challenges. She had to relocate the family frequently into less expensive housing.

While Elizabeth was discerning God's will for her future, the Virgin Mary became her prism of faith. In her discernment she relied on several advisors among the clergy, especially Rev. John Cheverus (1768-1836), the first bishop of Boston, and his associate Rev. Francis Matignon (1753-1818). After wrestling with doubts and fears in her search for truth, Elizabeth resolved her inner conflict regarding religious conversion and embraced Roman Catholicism.

Reverend Matthew O'Brien (1758-1815) received Elizabeth's profession of the Catholic faith at Saint Peter's Church, Barclay Street in lower Manhattan March 14, 1805. Elizabeth received her First Communion two weeks later on March 25th. Bishop John Carroll, whom she considered her spiritual father, confirmed her the next year on Pentecost Sunday. For her Confirmation name Elizabeth added the name of Mary to her own and thereafter frequently signed herself "MEAS," which was her abbreviation for Mary Elizabeth Ann Seton. Accordingly Elizabeth expressed that the three names, Mary, Ann, and Elizabeth, signified the moments of the mysteries of Salvation for her.

Elizabeth's initial years as a Catholic (1805-1808) in New York were marked by disappointments and failures. Rampant anti-Catholic prejudice prevented her from beginning her own school, so she secured a teaching position at the school of a Protestant couple, Mr. and Mrs. Patrick White, but they failed financially within a short time. Elizabeth's next venture was a boarding house for boys who attended a school directed by Rev. William Harris of Saint Mark's Episcopal Church, but disgruntled parents withdrew their sons. The Seton family also distrusted Elizabeth's influence on younger family members. Their fears were realized when Cecilia, her fifteen year-old sister-in-law, converted to Catholicism in 1806, later Harriet also made her profession of faith in 1809. During Cecilia's struggles as a new convert, Elizabeth wrote her an instructive *Spiritual Journal* in 1807 to offer wise counsel to the adolescent.

Although Elizabeth was frustrated in securing employment to provide for the welfare of her children, she remained faith-filled. She was convinced that God would show her the way according to the Divine Plan. All her life she believed that "God will provide, that is all my Comfort, never did that providence fail me."[6] In considering her future and examining alternatives, Elizabeth remained a mother first and foremost. She regarded her five "darlings" as her primary obligation over every other commitment.

Foundress—Maryland Mission

A priest of the Society of Saint Sulpice, Rev. Louis William Dubourg, S.S. (1766-1833), was visiting New York about 1806 when Elizabeth met him quite providentially. For about ten years Dubourg had desired to obtain a congregation of religious women to teach girls in Baltimore. He, with the concurrence of the first Catholic Bishop of the United States, John Carroll, invited Elizabeth to Baltimore with promise of assistance. Dubourg wished to form a small school for religious education of children. He assured Mrs. Seton that his confreres would assist her in forming a plan of life which would be in the best interests of her children.

After her arrival in Maryland, June 16, 1808, Elizabeth spent one year as a school mistress in Baltimore. Here the concept of the Sisters of Charity was conceived and the first steps taken towards realizing the Sulpicians' vision of education, formation, and ministry for the Church in the United States. This site is known as Saint Mary's Spiritual Center and Historic Site (see: stmarysspiritualcenter.org). Visitors are welcome.

The Society of Saint Sulpice (Sulpicians) were French émigré priests. They envisioned the development of a sisterhood modeled on the Daughters

[6] 6.142, Elizabeth Seton to Julia Scott, *Seton Collected Writings*, 2:256.

of Charity of Saint Vincent de Paul (founded 1633 in Paris). The priests actively recruited candidates for the germinal community. Cecilia Maria O'Conway (1788-1865), of Philadelphia, was the first to arrive December 7, 1808. She was followed in 1809 by others who wished to join Mrs. Seton in her endeavor: Mary Ann Butler (1784-1821) of Philadelphia; Susanna Clossey (1785-1823) of New York; Catharine Mullan (1783-1815) of Baltimore; Anna Maria Murphy Burke (c.1787-1812) of Philadelphia; and Rosetta (Rose) Landry White (1784-1841), a widow of Baltimore. Only Elizabeth pronounced private vows of chastity and obedience for one year to Archbishop John Carroll in the lower chapel at Saint Mary's Seminary, Paca Street March 25, 1809. On that occasion the Archbishop gave her the title "Mother Seton." The group of sisters appeared for the first time dressed alike in a black dress, cape, and white bonnet trimmed with a black band on June 16, 1809. Their attire was patterned after the dress worn by widows in Italy at the time Elizabeth stayed in that country.

Samuel Sutherland Cooper (1769-1843), a wealthy seminarian and convert, purchased 269 acres of land for an establishment for the sisterhood near Emmitsburg in the countryside of Frederick County, Maryland. Cooper wished to establish an institution for female education and character formation rooted in Christian values and the Catholic faith, as well as services to the elderly, job skill development, and a small manufactory, which would be beneficial to people living in poverty. Cooper had Elizabeth in mind to direct the educational program.

Emmitsburg Foundation

The stone farmhouse (c.1750) on the property was not yet ready for occupancy when Elizabeth and her first group arrived in the Emmitsburg environs mid-June 1809. Reverend John Dubois, S.S. (1764-1842), founder of Mount St. Mary's College and Seminary (1808), offered his cabin on St. Mary's Mountain for the women to use until they would be able to move to the valley below some six weeks later.

According to tradition, Elizabeth named the property surrounding her valley home Saint Joseph's Valley. There she founded her community. The Sisters of Charity of St. Joseph's began July 31, 1809, in the Stone House, the former Fleming farmhouse. Elizabeth and her companions moved into Saint Joseph's House (now the White House) February 20, 1810. They opened Saint Joseph's Free School February 22, 1810, to educate needy girls of the region. This was the first free Catholic school for girls staffed by sisters in the country. Saint Joseph's Academy began May 14, 1810, with the addition of boarding pupils who paid tuition which enabled the Sisters of Charity to subsidize their charitable mission. Saint Joseph's Academy and Free School formed the cradle of Catholic education in the United States.

During the first months in Saint Joseph's Valley, Mother Seton and her Sisters of Charity busied themselves with setting up housekeeping in their primitive farmhouse, creating a garden, tending animals for their livelihood, and getting acquainted with the local grocer, townsfolk, and farmers. They were about the business of beginning a new venture, forming a community in pioneer circumstances, and providing for their survival during the coming winter months. While making their first spiritual retreat, the eldest Seton boy became seriously ill when visiting his mother. His life was believed to be in danger for several weeks and he received the last sacraments. His mother nursed him in the Stone House, his aunt Harriet and Sister Rose White made a shroud and prepared everything to lay him out, as his death seemed imminent, but William recovered and returned to school at the mountain.

The sisters awaited the completion of their new log house in the fields which would be called Saint Joseph's House (the White House) and became the site of Saint Joseph's Free School and Academy. Not long afterwards Sister Cecilia Seton, whose health had always been fragile, alarmed everyone when she was taken ill but she, too, recovered. In the mysterious ways of God, Harriet Seton became gravely ill with a high fever and died unexpectedly at age twenty-one just three days before Christmas.

The Sulpicians assisted Elizabeth in adapting the seventeenth-century French *Common Rules of the Daughters of Charity* (1672) for the American Sisters of Charity in accord with the needs of the Catholic Church in the United States. Elizabeth formed her sisters in the Vincentian spirit according to the tradition of Louise de Marillac (1591-1660) and Vincent de Paul (1581-1660). Eighteen Sisters of Charity, including Elizabeth, made private, annual vows of poverty, chastity, obedience, and service of the poor for the first time July 19, 1813; thereafter they made vows annually on March 25th and lived by the *Regulations for the Society of Sisters of Charity in the United States of America* (1812).

Elected by the members of the community to be the first Mother of the Sisters of Charity, Elizabeth was reelected successively and remained the community leader until her death. The Sulpicians, who had conceived and founded the community, filled the ecclesiastical office of superior general through 1849. Elizabeth worked successively with three Sulpicians in this capacity: Rev. Louis William Dubourg, S.S., Rev. Jean-Baptiste David, S.S. (1761-1841), and Rev. John Dubois, S.S.

The Valley Home

Just after the approval of their rule, or way of life, Mother Seton's eldest daughter, Annina, who had been suffering from tuberculosis, died at age sixteen. Her loss was a severe cross which tested the mettle of Mother Seton's faith. Her spirit was seared with suffering, sacrifice, and sorrow which marked Mother Seton's twelve years at Emmitsburg from the beginning.

Divine Providence guided Elizabeth and her little community through the poverty and insecurity of their first years, yet numerous women joined the Sisters of Charity. Of the ninety-eight candidates who arrived during Elizabeth's lifetime, eighty-six of them actually joined the new community; seventy percent remained Sisters of Charity for life. Illness, sorrow, and early death were omnipresent in Elizabeth's life. She buried eighteen Sisters of Charity at Emmitsburg, in addition to her two daughters and her two sisters-in-law.

Once the rule was approved the sisters entered the first novitiate of the Sisters of Charity which opened February 2, 1812. When they completed their novitiate eighteen sisters pronounced annual vows of poverty, chastity, obedience, and service of the poor for the first time in the chapel of the Saint Joseph's House on the feast of Saint Vincent de Paul July 19, 1813. The following year a band of Sisters of Charity departed to make their first foundation beyond Saint Joseph's Valley. The ensuing five years were marked by community growth, expansion, ministry opportunities, and discussion about legal incorporation. In the midst of which Mother Seton nursed another gravely ill child and faced personal loss again as she cared for her youngest Rebecca whom she buried at the tender age of fourteen.

The Sisters of Charity intertwined social ministry with character formation in religious values and education in the faith in their ministries. Elizabeth sent sisters to Philadelphia in 1814 to manage Saint Joseph's Asylum, the first Catholic orphanage in the United States. The next year the Sisters of Charity made a foundation at Mount St. Mary's to oversee the infirmary and domestic services for the college and seminary near

Emmitsburg. A small band of sisters left Saint Joseph's Valley to make another foundation, the Roman Catholic Orphan Asylum (later Saint Patrick's Orphan Asylum) in New York City in 1817.

Woven among Elizabeth's grief and planning for new foundations were her own parental concerns about providing job training for her sons in order to prepare them for responsible adulthood. The mercantile firm of the Filicchi family in Livorno, Italy, provided opportunities for both William and Richard in turn, from 1817 through 1820. Yet, William longed for the high seas and a career in the United States Navy. Richard emulated his elder brother but opted to sail with the Navy as a civil servant. Their mother worried about them continually, counseling them about personal safety, fidelity to religious practices, and their own salvation. Similarly Elizabeth was concerned about the well-being and future circumstances of her only surviving daughter, Catherine Josephine, whom she sent to Philadelphia for a visit with Julianna Sitgreaves Scott (1765-1842). A life-long friend whom Elizabeth called Julia, was known to the Seton children as "Aunt Scott."

Julia Scott was like an elder sister and mentor to Elizabeth who was always delighted to receive a "precious letter" from her dear friend for so many years. In her reply, Elizabeth conveyed her inner self to Julia who had recently been widowed and returned to her native Philadelphia: "I tell you from my Heart, that you are inexpressibly dear to It—that I would give the greatest share of any good I enjoy to add to your comfort, but what I most desire and wish for you now is Peace—that first and most perfect of all earthly attainments."[7]

Despite declining health Mother Seton continued her direction and formation of the Sisters of Charity and the handling of matters of parents, pupils, and business related to Saint Joseph's Academy and Free School. Voluminous correspondence, instructions, and translations occupied her along with day-to-day community life in the Valley. In late October 1820 Elizabeth went to the construction site of a new building for day pupils to survey its status. When she climbed a pile of boards, a very sharp west wind swept around her. A result was the onset of illness, high fever, and a sharp decline in health. Within a few days Mother Seton received the last sacraments but she did not go to her eternal reward for another two months, January 4, 1821.

---

[7] 1.16, Elizabeth Seton to Julia Scott, 23 April 1798, *Seton Collected Writings*, 1:25.

Relational Spirituality

Saint Elizabeth Ann Seton in all her life roles, whether as Betty Bayley, Mrs. William Magee Seton, or Mother Seton, lived the life of both Martha and Mary.[8] By virtue of personality, Elizabeth was more inclined to introspection and reflection but life roles called her to action and service. She nurtured many intimate friendships, some of which had deep religious dimensions. She walked with others and was accompanied herself along spiritual pathways, both as director and directee. She sought and listened for God's will to be manifested through spiritual advisors. Elizabeth considered Archbishop John Carroll as her spiritual father and looked to him as an oracle of God's plan for her. While her sister-in-law Rebecca Seton was her soul's sister during her years as an Episcopalian in New York, members of the Filicchi family were God's instruments in introducing Elizabeth to Roman Catholicism. Yet it was probably Rev. Simon Gabriel Bruté, a Sulpician priest and her confessor at Emmitsburg during her last years, who understood her soul best and was responsive to its array of mystical musings.

How Elizabeth lived her vocations as wife, mother, and religious woman illustrates the degree to which she balanced her prayer life with apostolic zeal. This integration had its lifeline in a vibrant relational spirituality, which nourished her entire being and enabled her to be present to God, self, and others as a woman of faith.

Psalm 23 was pivotal in Elizabeth's relationship with God along with Sacred Scripture, the Eucharist, and Mary. Elizabeth discovered the Mother of God in 1803, while she was in Italy, where she began her search for truth. Mary became a focus of faith during her study, discernment, and religious conversion. Elizabeth's spirituality was Biblical, Eucharistic, Incarnational, and rooted in events which communicated God's will. She listened and acted on the Word of God and became a loyal daughter of the Church after her conversion to Roman Catholicism in 1805.

The roots of Elizabeth's sanctity are in her own early formation in the Protestant Episcopal Church of the Bayley and Charlton families from whom she first learned about God's love and developed a trust in Divine Providence. Elizabeth deepened her understanding of herself as a child of God through her experience of being loved in her own family and also through meanderings among nature, whether along the seashore, in the

---

[8] Cf. Luke 10:38-42.

12

woods, or in meadows. These gave her food for thoughtful reflection and inspired journaling about her experiences and feelings. From youth through adulthood, Elizabeth nourished herself with poetry, reading, and music. Her inner sense of the sacred was heightened amidst the pomp and splendor of religious devotions, ceremonies, chant, and artwork encountered in Italy which fueled her inquiry into questions of faith and salvation. She longed for Eternity and union with God.

As a faith-filled woman, Elizabeth not only reached out to relatives, neighbors, and poor widows in times of loneliness, sickness, and hardship, but also encouraged others to do so. In addition to nurturing her own children, through her attentive listening, kindness, and advice, Elizabeth engaged in meaningful conversation, correspondence, and religious instruction of others whether peers, companions, parents, or pupils. She lived her baptismal consecration and her religious commitment as one who embraced her cross, willing to live the Paschal Mystery in her own life. She was a woman of indomitable faith and indefatigable charity. Her life-long commitment to education and religious instruction testifies to her thirst for mercy and justice particularly for children from families living in poverty. She recognized that education provides an avenue out of poverty.

Friendship Circle

The sphere of Elizabeth's relationships widened like a spiral throughout her life. Her friendships with Julia Sitgreaves Scott, Eliza Craig Sadler, and Catherine Mann Dupleix are paramount. Despite changes of circumstances, religious conversion, and vocational choices, each corresponded with Elizabeth, providing emotional support during times of turmoil and crisis. Julia Scott also provided financial support regularly after Elizabeth was widowed. Their correspondence reflects the comfort and understanding between women, mothers, and widows who shared a mutual bond of friendship.

Through her marriage to William Magee Seton in 1794 Elizabeth came to know his younger siblings, particularly Rebecca Mary Seton, who was the oldest unmarried Seton girl. The two young women became fast friends, spiritual companions, and women of charity as members of the *Society to Aid Poor Widows with Young Children*. As a result of the Setons' voyage to Italy for the restoration of William Magee's health, Elizabeth meticulously penned a record for her sister-in-law about their adventure and his condition.

Elizabeth became acquainted with the Filicchi family of Livorno, whom William Magee knew when his father sent him to visit major European ports and mercantile establishments. Fifteen years later the Filicchi family provided gracious hospitality to him, his wife and daughter. Elizabeth's ongoing friendship with all members of the Filicchi family was life-changing as she described her religious conversion in a journal written to Amabilia Baragazzi Filicchi.

Upon her return to the United States, Elizabeth compared religions in an attempt to discern the true one founded by Jesus Christ. Her circle of counselors and correspondents widened prior to her conversion to include not only John Carroll, but also Rev. Jean Cheverus and Rev. Francis Matignon. After 1805, Rev. Jean Tisserant and Rev. Louis William Dubourg, S.S., were added to her circle of clergy, consultants, and spiritual advisors.

After establishing the Sisters of Charity of St. Joseph's, Elizabeth's horizon expanded to include the wisdom of other Sulpician priests like Rev. Charles Nagot, S.S., Rev. Pierre Babade, S.S., Rev. John Dubois, S.S., and Rev. Simon G. Bruté, S.S. Elizabeth also corresponded with the parents of her pupils, including Matthias O'Conway of Philadelphia, and Mrs. William Raborg. She also kept in touch, directly or indirectly, through correspondence with Sisters of Charity located in Philadelphia and New York, particularly like Sister Rose White, Sister Cecilia O'Conway, and Sister Margaret George. She also mentions other sisters in letters and sends them messages. In truth Elizabeth supplied the hand of real friendship to everyone associated with her endeavors.

On Family—to Rebecca Seton

Rebecca Mary Seton (1780-1804) was the second daughter of William and Anna Maria Curzon Seton. Elizabeth discovered her sister-in-law to be a woman of virtue and talent. The pair became dear friends and confidants. The two were active in social ministry projects through Trinity Episcopal Church and the *Society to Aid Poor Widows with Small Children*. For this reason, they were sometimes called "Protestant Sisters of Charity." Elizabeth often referred to Rebecca as her "soul sister." After the death of William Seton, Sr., Rebecca assisted Elizabeth with instruction of the younger Seton girls (Mary, Charlotte, Harriet, and Cecilia), ranging from fourteen to eight years of age.

When Elizabeth accompanied William Magee Seton to Italy, Rebecca assumed responsibility for care of three of the children, William (7), Richard (6), and Catherine (3). Rebecca and her charges stayed with the family of an older brother, James Seton and Eliza Maitland. The Seton family was prone to tuberculosis. While the Setons were away in Italy, Rebecca became gravely ill and was unable to meet her beloved sister-in-law at the wharf when Elizabeth and her daughter returned to New York. Elizabeth rushed to Rebecca's bedside and was with her when she died some weeks later on July 8.

The following journal was written by Elizabeth Seton for her dear Rebecca in 1803 and 1804. The entries of this nine month period are but a sample of over seventy letters between dear friends who were also sisters-in-law. Elizabeth shared with Rebecca the heartache of their ordeal of being quarantined, William Magee's illness and death, and her religious experiences in Tuscany.

Quarantine Station, Staten Island[1]

2nd October 1803

My dearest Sister—

My Soul's Sister—We are quietly seated at dear Joseph Bayley's,[2] and are not to go to sea until 10 o'clock tomorrow—Our Willy[3] felt the passing our Battery so much that I scarcely dared wave my dear red handkerchief— but since then he has been very composed and better than on shore—My heart is lifted, feels *its treasure*[4] and the little cabin and my cross are objects of peace and sweet comfort—He is with me and what can I fear—ten thousand loves to my darlings and most to my dear girls—

I shall write you by Henry Seton[5]—who will tell you I have had a ravenous appetite and have been very cheerful—Your being sick is my greatest care—but that, too, must be referred to Our All Sufficient God.

My Friend and Brother's deserted dwelling started my first tear—the dear study windows were all I could see—

Your own, *Sis*

Page is to keep Mrs. McDugal's letter till Mrs. Vanduzer[6] sends for it—

&ﻬ&ﻬ&ﻬ

New Light House, 12 O'clock[7]

3rd October 1803

My dearest Rebecca—

Our William is quite easy without stricture of the breast, fever, or cough in any great degree, or sweat as much as usual, but slept very well from 7 to eleven, and from 11:30 until 3:30—He has more appetite than I

---

[1] 1.178, *Seton Collected Writings,* 1:225.

[2] Dr. Joseph Bayley had been an assistant to Dr. Richard Bayley.

[3] William Magee Seton reacted emotionally at seeing their home on State Street as the ship sailed from New York.

[4] The Bible, religious books, and notes which Elizabeth had brought with her on the voyage.

[5] Elizabeth's brother-in-law who would be returning to New York.

[6] The VanDuzer (or VanDusen) family on Staten Island had a farm, sold provisions, and ran a ferry, which probably carried mail.

[7] 2.1, *Seton Collected Writings,* 1:243.

wish as it brings on fever invariably—but as he certainly is even now stronger than when he left home, I trust that will soon wear off—Anna has been very sick but after relieving her stomach, has fallen asleep. Mrs. O'Brien and her child are also in their berth and Willy is pondering over his molasses and spoon not very well able to keep his legs, but not at all sick—I am as usual, sober and quiet, made my breakfast with a great relish and it still sets very comfortably—

I feel so satisfied in my hidden treasure that you might think me an old rock—Mr. and Mrs. O'Brien[8] are really kind friends to us. The steward seems as anxious to please me as even our Mary[9] could be—and a dear little child about 18 months makes me sigh for Tatle Beck.[10] As I told Joseph Bayley, "I neither look behind nor before, only up, there is my rest, and I want nothing."

—one o'clock—Henry Seton is leaving us, all goes well—the Lord on high is mightiest—they threaten a storm—but I fear not with Him—

Your *EAS.*

Bless my darling Girls[11] for me and many loves to my little ones—

ৡৢৡৢৡৢ

8th November in Gibraltar Bay[12]

Was climbing with great difficulty a mountain of immense height and blackness when near the top, almost exhausted a voice said: "Never mind, take courage there is a beautiful green hill on the other side—and on it an angel waits for you." (at that moment Willy woke me to help him)

Said to me—now we will part no more in time nor in Eternity—No more repeated on who held by the hand in time nor in Eternity—

---

[8] Mrs. O'Brien was the wife of the captain of *The Shepherdess*, the ship on which the Setons sailed to Italy.

[9] Probably a woman who worked for the Setons in their household.

[10] "Tatle Beck," "Little Tat," or "Tate" are forms of family nick-names for the toddler Rebecca.

[11] The Setons provided for the younger half-sisters of William Magee Seton (Charlotte, Mary, Harriet, and Cecilia), as well as their own children. William, Richard, and Catherine were left in the care of Rebecca Seton (1780-1804). Their infant Rebecca was staying with Elizabeth's own sister, Mary Bayley Post and her family.

[12] 2.5, *Seton Collected Writings*, 1:246.

8th November Mrs. M ill in great distress—

Can I ever forget the setting sun over the little Island of Ibiza?[13]

11th November 1803—6 o'clock Evening

My dear little Anna shed many tears on her prayer book over the 92nd Psalm in consequence of my telling her that we offended God every day. Our conversation began by her asking me "if God put down our bad actions in His book as well as our good ones?"

She said she wondered how anyone could be sorry to see a dear baby die—She thought there was more cause to cry when they were born.

Considering the infirmity and corrupt nature which would overpower the Spirit of Grace, and the enormity of the offense to which the least indulgence of them would lead me—in the anguish of my soul shuddering to offend my Adored Lord—I have this day solemnly engaged that through the strength of His Holy Spirit, I will not again expose that corrupt and infirm nature to the smallest temptation which I can avoid. Therefore if my Heavenly Father will once more reunite us all that I will make a daily sacrifice of every wish even the most innocent, least they should betray me to a deviation from the solemn and sacred vow I have now made—

O my God, imprint it on my soul with the strength of Thy Holy Spirit that by His Grace, supported and defended, I may never more forget that Thou are my All, and that I cannot be received in Thy Heavenly Kingdom without a pure and faithful heart supremely devoted to Thy Holy Will. O keep me for the sake of Jesus Christ.

Shepherdess—14th November 1803

15th November

A heavy storm of thunder and lightning at midnight—my soul assured and strong in its Almighty Protector, encouraged itself in Him, while the knees trembled as they bent to Him.

The worm of the dust writhing at the terrors of its Almighty Judge—a helpless child clinging to the Mercy of its Tender Father— A redeemed soul strong in the strength of its Adored Saviour—

After reading a great deal and long and earnest prayer went to bed—but could not rest—a little voice (my own Anna who I thought was

[13] The island of Ibiza, part of the Baleraic group of islands off the southeast coast of Spain.

asleep) in a soft whisper said "Come hither all ye weary souls." I changed my place to her arms—the rocking of the vessel and breaking of the waves were forgot—the heavy sighs and restless pains were lost in a sweet refreshing sleep—

Adored Redeemer it was Thy Word, by the voice of one of thy little ones, who promises indeed to be one of thy Angels—

November 18th while the Ave Maria[14] bells were ringing arrived in the mole of Leghorn [Livorno]—

19th Towed by a 14 oared barge to the San Jacopo Lazaretto Prison.[15] When we entered our room, Anna viewed the high arches, naked walls and brick floor, with streaming eyes, and as soon as her Father was composed on his mattress and they had bolted and barred us in this immense place alone for the night, clinging round my neck and bursting again in tears she said, "If Papa should die here, Mamma, God will be with us."

22nd Sung our evening hymns again with little Anna. She said while we were looking at the setting sun, "Mamma I dreamed last night that two men had hold of me to kill me, and as one had struck my breast with a knife, in that instant I awoke, and found myself safe. I was thinking that so it will be with my Soul, while I am struggling with Death, in an instant I shall awake and find myself safe from all that I feared—but then FOREVER"—our Jesus !!!

❧❧❧❧❧❧

19th November 1803, 10 o'clock at night[16]

How eagerly would you listen to the voice that should offer to tell you where your "dear Sis" is now—your Soul's Sister, yet you could not rest in your bed if you saw her as she is—sitting in one corner of an immense prison—locked in and barred with as much ceremony as any monster of mischief might be—a single window, double grated with iron through which, if I should want anything, I am to call a sentinel with a fierce cocked hat and long rifle—gun, that is, that he may not receive the dreadful infection (yellow fever) we are supposed to have brought from New York.

---

[14] This probably refers to the bells which are pealed at morning, noon, and evening in Catholic churches for the Angelus, a prayer in honor of Mary, which includes the Hail Mary (Ave Maria, in Latin).

[15] A lazaretto is a place of quarantine.

[16] 2.6, *Seton Collected Writings*, 1:249. Elizabeth Seton also described these experiences of December 4 in a subsequent letter. See 2.7, *Ibid.*, 1:266.

To commence from where I left you last night—I went to sleep and dreamed I was in the middle aisle of Trinity Church,[17] singing with all my soul, the hymns at our dear Sacrament. So much comfort made me more than satisfied, and when I heard in the morning a boat was along side of our ship, I flew on deck and would have thrown myself in the arms of dear Guy Carleton,[18] but he retired from me and a guard whom I saw for the first time said "don't touch." It now was explained that our ship was the first to bring the news of yellow fever in New York, which our lack of a Bill of Health[19] discovered, that the pilot who brought us into the mole must lose his head. Our ship must go out in the roads and my poor William, being ill, must go with his baggage to the lazaretto. At this moment the band of music that welcomes strangers came under our cabin windows and played, "Hail Columbia" and all those little tunes that set the darlings singing and dancing at home.

Mrs. O'Brien and the rest were half wild with joy, but I was glad to hide in my berth the full heart of sorrow which seemed as if it must break. Do not judge me! You can never have an idea of the looks and tears of my poor Willy, who seemed as if he would not live over the day.

Presently appeared a boat with 14 oars. We hurried in another, with only one change of clothes, as they promised we should have the rest on Monday, and the lazaretto being some miles out of the town, we were towed out to sea again, and after an hour's ride over the waves, the chains which are across the entrance of the canal, which leads to this place were let loose.

December 4th The printed word—my Bible, commentaries, Kempis,[20] visible, and in continual enjoyment—When I cannot get hours, I take minutes—Invisible, oh the company is numberless—sometimes I feel so assured that the Guardian Angel is immediately present that I look up from my book and can hardly persuade myself I am not touched. "Poor soul!" my John Henry Hobart would say.

"She will lose her reason in that Prison!"—more than that I sometimes feel that his angel is near and undertake to converse with it—but

---

[17] The Setons were Protestant Episcopalians who belonged to Trinity Church in New York.
[18] Guy Carleton Bayley (1786-1859), the youngest son of Dr. Richard and Charlotte Barclay Bayley and half-brother of Elizabeth Seton, was employed by the Filicchi firm in Livorno.
[19] Medical clearance for a vessel assuring that all passengers are free of communicable disease.
[20] Thomas à Kempis, a fifteenth-century writer, authored the classic devotional *The Imitation of Christ*, which Elizabeth enjoyed for spiritual reading.

these enjoyments only come when all is quiet and I have passed an hour or two with King David, the prophet Isaiah, or become spiritually elevated by some of the commentaries—

These hours, I often think, I shall hereafter wish to recall more than any of my life—

My Father and my God—Who by the consoling voice of his Word builds up the soul in hope so as to free it even for hours of its encumbrances—confirming and strengthening it by the hourly experience of His indulgent goodness—giving it a new life in Him even while in the midst of sorrows and care—sustaining, directing, consoling and blessing through every changing scene of its pilgrimage—making His Will its guide to temporal comfort and eternal glory. How shall this most unwearied diligence, the most cheerful compliance, the most humble resignation ever express enough my love, my joy, thanksgiving and praise?

❧❧❧❧❧❧

19th November 1803—10 o'clock at night [continued][21]

...To commence from where I left off last night—...The Lazaretto being some miles from the town we were towed out to sea again, and after an hour's ride over the waves, the chains which cross the entrance of the canal which leads to this place were let down at the signal of several successive bells, and after another row between walls as high as our second story windows and the quarrelling and the hallooing of the waterman where we should be landed, the boat stopped.

Another succession of bells brought down one guard after another, and in about half an hour Monsieur le Capitano[22]—who after much whispering and consultation with his lieutenant said we might come out, upon which every one retreated and a guard pointed with his bayonet the way which we were to go. An order from the commandant was sent from our boat to the Capitano which was received on the end of a stick. They were obliged to light a fire to smoke it before it would be read. My books always go with me, and they were carefully put up—but must all be looked over and the papers in the little secretary examined. The person who did this and

---

[21] 2.7 *Seton Collected Writings*, 1:251. Possibly fatigue caused Elizabeth Seton to repeat some of the same details which she had written previously (cf. 2.6). Duplications have been omitted here for the convenience of readers.

[22] A captain in the Italian military who was a guard at the San Jacopo Lazaretto.

examined our mattresses must perform as long a quarantine as ourselves. Poor little Anna, how she trembled, and William tottered along as if every moment he must fall which had he done, no one dared for their life to touch him. We were directed to go opposite to the window of the Capitano's house in which sat Mrs. Filippo Filicchi[23], in such a style—but hush compliments and kind looks without number. A fence was between us but I fear did not hide my fatigue both of soul and body. First we had chairs handed, rather placed for us—for the chairs, after we had touched them, could not go back to the house. At length we were shown the door we should enter No. 6—up 20 stone steps, a room with high arched ceilings like Saint Paul's[24]—brick floor, naked walls and a jug of water. The Capitano sent 3 warm eggs, a bottle of wine and some slips of bread. Willy's mattress was soon spread, and he upon it. He could neither touch wine nor eggs—our little syrups, currant jelly, drinks etc., which he must have every half hour on board ship. Where were they? I had heard the Lazaretto, the very place for comfort for the sick—and brought nothing.

I soon found there was a little closet, on which my knees found rest, and after emptying my heart and washing the bricks with my tears returned to my poor Willy, and found him and Anna both in want of a preacher. Dear puss she soon found a rope that had tied her box and began jumping away to warm herself, for the coldness of the bricks and walls made us shiver. A sunset dinner came from the Filicchis[25] with other necessaries. We went to the grate again to see them.

Now on the ship [with] mattresses spread on this cool floor, my Willy and Anna are sound asleep. I trust that God who has given him strength to go through a day of such exertion will carry us on. He is our all indeed! My eyes smart so much with crying, wind, and fatigue that I must close them and lift up my heart. Sleep won't come very easily. If you had seen little Anna's arms clasped round my neck at her prayers, while the tears rolled a stream, how you would love her. I read her to sleep—little pieces of trust in God—she said "Mamma, if Papa should die here—but God will be

---

[23] Mary Cowper Filicchi (1760-1821) of Boston was the wife of Filippo Filicchi.

[24] Elizabeth also worshipped at Saint Paul's Church in New York.

[25] There were two Filicchi brothers: Filippo and Antonio. Filippo (1763-1816) had spent time in the United States (1785-86). Antonio (1764-1847), whom William Magee had known during his apprenticeship with the family firm, was married to Amabilia Baragazzi (1773-1853). Both families were gracious in welcoming the Setons and providing hospitality to Elizabeth Seton.

with us."[26] God is with us—and if sufferings abound in us, His consolations also greatly abound, and far exceed all utterance.[27]

If the wind that now almost puts out my light and blows on my Willy through every crevice and over our chimney like loud thunder, could come from any but His Command—or if the circumstances that has placed us in so forlorn a situation were not guided by His Hand—miserable indeed would be our case. Within the hour Willy has had a violent fit of coughing so as to bring up blood which agitates and distresses him through all his endeavors to hide it.

What shall we say? This is the hour of trial. The Lord support and strengthen us in it. Retrospections bring anguish—press forward toward the mark and prize—

20th Sunday morning The Matins[28] bells awakened my Soul to its most painful regrets and filled it with an agony of sorrow which could not at first find relief, even in prayer. In the little closet from whence there is a view of the open sea, and the beatings of the waves against the high rocks at the entrance of this prison which throws them violently back and raises the white foam as high as its walls, I first came to my senses and reflected that I was offending my only Friend and Resource in my misery and voluntarily shutting out from my soul the only consolation it could receive—pleading for mercy and strength brought peace. With a cheerful countenance, I asked Will what we should do for breakfast—the doors were unbarred and a bottle of milk set down in the entrance of the room. Little Anna and Will ate it with bread, and I walked the floor with a crust and glass of wine.

Will could not sit up. His ague came on and my soul's agony with it. My husband on the cold bricks without fire, shivering and groaning—lifting his dim and sorrowful eyes, with a fixed gaze in my face while his tears ran on his pillow without one word. Anna rubbed one hand and I the other till his fever came on. The Capitano who brought us news that our time was lessened five days, told me to be satisfied with the dispensations of God etc., and was answered by such a succession of sobs, that he soon departed. Mr. Filicchi now came to comfort my Willy. When he went away, we said as

---

[26] Cf. 2 John 1:3.
[27] Cf. 2 Cor. 1:5.
[28] Church bells announcing the pre-dawn liturgical office.

much of our Blessed Service[29] as Will could go through. I then was obliged to lay my head down. Dinner was sent from town and a servant to stay with us during our quarantine—Louie—an old man, very little—grey hair and blue eyes, which changed their expressions from joy to sorrow, as if they would console and still enliven. My face was covered with a handkerchief when he came in and tired of the sight of men with cocked hats, cockades and bayonets, I did not look up. Poor Louis, how long shall I remember his voice of sorrow and tenderness, when refusing the dinner, he looked up with lifted hands in some prayer that God would comfort me. I was comforted when I did not look at my poor Will but to see him as he then was worse than to see him dead.

And now the bolts of another door were hammered open and Louis who has become an object of equal terror (along with ourselves) having entered our room and touched what we had touched, had an apartment allotted him. How many times did the poor old man run up and down the nearly perpendicular 20 steps to get things necessary for our comfort next morning. When all was done I handed him a chair that he might rest—he jumped almost over it and danced round me like a madman, declaring he would work all night to serve us. My Will, so wearied out, was soon asleep. Anna with a flood of tears prayed a blessing and soon forgot her sorrows. It seemed as if opening my Prayer Book and bending my knees was the signal for my soul to find rest. It was 9 o'clock with us—3 o'clock at home in New York. I imagined what I had so often enjoyed and consoled myself with the thought that although separated in the body six thousand miles,[30] my soul and the souls I love were at the Throne of Grace at the same time, in the same prayers, to one Almighty Father accepted through our Adored Redeemer and enlightened by one Blessed Spirit. Then did my soul "rejoice indeed in the Lord and Triumph in the God of its Salvation." After prayers, I read my little book of dear Henry Hobart's sermons, and became far more happy then I had been wretched. I went to bed at 12 but got up twice to prayers—and to help my poor Willy.

Monday—Awoke with the same rest and comfort with which I had laid down. Gave my Will his warm milk and began to consider our

---

[29] The Setons were Protestant Episcopalians whose worship service followed an order found in the *Book of Common Prayer*, based on the Bible. Every worship service included the reading of sacred texts from the Hebrew and Christian Scriptures.
[30] Round trip between Italy and New York across the Atlantic.

situation although so unfavorable to his condition as one of the steps in the dispensations of that Almighty Will which could alone choose aright for us. Set Anna to work and myself to the dear Scriptures as usual—laying close behind the dear shiverer to keep him from the ague.[31] Our Capitano came with his guards and put up a very neat bed and curtains sent by Filicchi—and fixed the benches on which Anna and I were to lie. Took down our names: Signor Guglielmo, Signora Elizabeth and Signorina Anna Maria. The voice of kindness which again entreated me to look up to "le bon Dieu" made me look up to the speaker and in our Capitano I found every expression of a benevolent heart. His great cocked hat being off, I found it had hidden grey hair and a kind and affectionate countenance. "I had a wife. I loved her—I loved her. Oh! She gave me a daughter which she commended to my care—and died." He clasped his hands and looked up—and then at my Will. "If God calls, what can we do, et que voulez vous Signora."[32] I began to love my Capitano—

Read and jumped the rope to warm me; looked round our prison and found that its situation was beautiful. I comforted my Will all I could by rubbing his hands and wiping his tears, and giving words of faith to his soul, which was too weak to pray for itself. I heard Anna read while I watched the setting sun in a cloud. After both were asleep, I read, prayed, wept, and prayed again until eleven o'clock. We were at no loss to know the hours—night and day four bells strike every hour and ring every quarter.

Tuesday—My Will was better and very much encouraged by his Dr. Tutilli,[33] who was very kind to him—also our Capitano who now seemed to understand me a little and who again repeated "I loved My Wife. I loved her and she died et que voulez vous Signora."

I talked with the Filicchis at the grate and with great difficulty got my Will up the steps again, nursed him, read to him—heard Anna—and made the most of our troubles. Our Louie brought us an elegant bouquet, Jasmine, Geranium, Pinks, etc. He makes excellent soup—cooks all with charcoal in little earthen pots. No sunset but a heavy gale which, if anything could move our wills, would certainly bring them down. The roaring of the sea sounds like thunder.

---

[31] The onset of a fever along with recurring chills, fever, and sweating.
[32] Literally, "What do you wish, Madame?"
[33] Dr. Tutilli was an Italian physician retained by the Filicchi family to attend William Magee Seton in San Jacopo Lazaretto.

Passed my evening as the last—quite reconciled to the sentinels' watch and bolts and bars. I'm not afraid of my candle, as the window shutter is the only piece of wood about us.

Wednesday—Not only willing to take my cross but kissed it too—and whilst glorying in our consolations, my poor Will was taken with an ague which was almost too much. He told me as he often had done before, that it was too late. His strength was going from him every hour and he should go gradually—but not long—this to me—to his friends quite cheerful. He was not able to go to them, they were admitted to our door but must not touch the least thing near us. A point of our Capitano's stick warded Willy off when in eager conversation he would go too near. It reminded me of going to see the lions. One of the guards brought a pot of incense also to purify our air.

Quiet half-hour at sunset. Anna and I sang Advent[34] hymns with low voice. Oh—after all were asleep, I said our dear Worship Service alone. Willy had not been able in the day. I found heavenly consolation, forgot prisons, bolts and sorrow, and would have rejoiced to have sung with Paul and Silas.[35]

Thursday—I find my present opportunity a treasure—and my confinement of body [provides] a liberty of soul which I may never again enjoy whilst they are united. Every moment not spent with my dear books, or in my nursing duty, is a loss. Anna is so happy with her rag baby and little presents it is a pleasure to see her. Our Capitano brought us news that another five days were granted, and the 19th of December we would be free. Poor Willy says with a groan, "I believe before then." We pray and cry together, till fatigue overpowers him, and then he says he is willing to go to God—cheering up is useless. He seems easier after venting his sorrow and always gets quiet sleep after his struggles. A heavy storm of wind which drives the spray from the sea against our window adds to his melancholy. If I could forget my God one moment at these times I should go mad, but He hushes all—"Be still and know that I am God your Father."[36]

Dear home, dearest Sisters, my little ones—WELL—either protected by God in this world—or in Heaven. It is a sweet thought to dwell on, that all those I most tenderly love—love God—and if we do not meet again

[34] A period of religious preparation for Christmas.
[35] Paul of Tarsus and Silas rejoice even though in prison in Philippi. See Acts 16:25.
[36] Cf. Ps. 46:10.

here—there we shall be separated no more. If I have lost them now, their gain is infinite and eternal. How often I tell my Will "when you awake in that world you will find that nothing could tempt you to return to this. You will see that your care over your wife and little ones, was like a hand only to hold the cup which God himself will give if He takes you."

Heavenly Father, pity the weak and burdened souls of Thy poor creatures, who have not strength to look to Thee, and lift us from the dust for His sake, our resurrection and our Life Jesus Christ, our Adored Redeemer.

Friday—November 25. A day of bodily pain, but peace in God—Knelt on our mattresses round the little table and said our dear Service. The storm of wind was so great! Guy Carleton was admitted at the foot of the stairs, and from the top I conversed with him which is always a great pleasure as he seems to me next to an angel. I ventured to remind my poor Will that it was our darling William's birthday, which cost him many tears. He also cried over our dear Harriet Seton's profile. Indeed he is so weak that even a thought of home makes him shed tears. How gracious is the Lord who strengthens my poor soul. Consider my husband who left his all to seek a milder climate, confined in this place of high and damp walls exposed to cold and wind which penetrates to the very bones, without fire except the kitchen charcoal, which oppresses his breast so much as to nearly convulse him. No little syrup nor softener of the cough, bark and milk, bitter tea, and opium pills which he takes quietly as a duty without seeming even to hope, is all I can offer him from day to day. When nature fails, and I can no longer look up with cheerfulness, I hide my head on the chair by his bedside and he thinks I am praying—and pray I do—for prayer is all my comfort, without which I should be of little service to him. Night and day he calls me "his life, his soul, his dearest of women—his all."

Our Capitano came this afternoon and seeing poor Willy in a high fever said: "in this room, what suffering have I seen. There, lay an Armenian begging a knife to end the struggles of death. There where the Signora's bed is, in the frenzy of fever a Frenchman insisted on shooting himself, and died in agony." Little notes of paper pasted on the doors mark how many days different persons have stayed and the shutter is all over notched—10—20—30—40 days. I do not mark ours—trusting they are marked above—He only knows best. Dear, dear William I can sometimes inspire him for a few minutes to feel that it would be sweet to die. He always says "My Father and my God, Thy will be done." Our Father in pity and compassion—Our God is in power to aid and to save—Who promises to pardon and receive us through our Adored Redeemer, Who will not let those perish for whom He has shed his Precious Blood.

Only to reflect—If we did not now know and love God—If we did not feel the consolations, and embrace the cheering hope He has set before us, and find our delight in the study of his Blessed Word and Truth, what would become of us?

> "Though torn from Nature's most endearing ties,
> The hearts warm hope, and love's maternal glow
> Though sunk the Source on which the Soul relies
> To soothe through life's decline its destin'd woe
> Though Sorrow still affecting ills prepares
> And o'er each passing day her presence lowers
> And darkened Fancy shades with many cares
> With many trials crowds the future hours
> Still in the Lord will I rejoice
> Still in my God I lift my voice
> Father of Mercies! still my grateful lays
> Shall hymn Thy Name, exulting in Thy Praise."[37]

Capitano says "all religions are good. It is good to keep one's own, but yours is as good as mine, to 'do to others as you would wish them to do to you'[38] that is all religion and the only point." "Tell me, dear Capitano, do you take this as a good principle only or also as a command?" "I reverence the command, Signora" "Well, Monsieur le Capitano, He who commanded your excellent rule, also commanded in the first place, 'Love the Lord your God with all your Soul.' Do you not give that the first place Capitano?" "Ah Signora, it is excellent—mais il y a tant de choses."[39] Poor Capitano! Sixty years of age and yet to find that to give God the soul interferes with "so many things."

Dear little Anna—"the child shall die a hundred years old—and the Sinner a hundred years shall be—lost."

---

[37] The source of this verse or hymn is unidentified. Its last four lines may reflect Elizabeth's daily recitation of Psalm 118.

[38] Matthew 7:12.

[39] "But there are so many things."

Tuesday, 29th November. I was obliged to go to bed at 10 last night to get warm in little Anna's arm. Awoke this morning while the moon was setting opposite our window but could not enjoy its brightness as the spray from the sea keeps the glass always thick. Laid in Bed till 9 with little Anna to explain to her our tedium. She said "one thing always troubles me, Mamma—Christ says they who would reign with Him must suffer with Him—and if I was now cut off, where should I go for I have not yet suffered." She coughs very much with a great deal of pain in her breast. She said "sometimes I think when this pain comes in my breast, that God will call me soon and take me from this world where I am always offending him, and how good that would be, if he gives me a sickness that I may bear patiently, that I may try and please Him." I explained to my Anna "you please Him every day when you help me through my troubles." "O do I Mamma? Thank God! Thank God!"

After breakfast read our Psalms and the 15th Chapter of Isaiah to my Will with so much delight that it made us all merry. He read at little Anna's request the last chapter of Revelations, but the tones of his voice, no heart can stand.

A storm of wind still—and very cold. Willy with a blanket over his shoulders creeps to the old man's fire. Anna jumps the rope, and I hop on one foot five or six times the length of the room without stopping. Laugh at me, my Sister, but it is very good exercise, and warms sooner than a fire when there is a warm heart to set it in motion.

Sang hymns—read promises to My Willy shivering under the bed clothes—and felt that the Lord is with us—and that He is our All—

The fever comes hot—the bed shakes even with his breathing—My God, my Father!

Saint Andrew—30th November 1803. William again by the kitchen fire—last night 30 or 40 poor souls of all nations: Turks, Greeks, Spaniards, and Frenchmen, arrived here from a shipwreck. They had no mattresses, clothes, or food—great coats without shirts—shirts without coats—these sent all to one room with naked walls, and the jug of water—until the commandant should find leisure to supply them. Our Capitano says he can do nothing without orders. "Pátiencé—que voulez vous Signora." Anna says, "for all we are so cold, and in this prison, Mamma, how happy we are compared with them; and we have peace, too. They quarrel, fight, and halloo all the time. The Capitano sends us even chestnuts and fruits from his own table. Those have not Bread." Dear Anna, you will see many more such mysteries.

At Willy's bedside, we have said our daily Service. He thought it would stop his shivering. My William's soul is so humble it will hardly embrace that faith which is its only resource. At any time whom have we but Our Redeemer, but when the spirit is on the brink of departure it must cling to Him with increased force or where is it?

Dear Will, it is not from the impulse of terror you seek your God, you tried and wished to serve Him long before this trial came. Why then will you not consider Him as the Father who knows all the different means and dispositions of His children and will graciously receive those who come to him by that way which He has appointed? You say your only hope is in Christ, what other hope do we need?

He says that the first effect he ever felt from the calls of the Gospel he experienced from our dear Henry Hobart's pressing the question in one of his sermons. "What avails gaining the whole world and losing your own Soul?"[40] The reflections he made when he returned home were "I toil and toil and what is it, what I gain, destroys me daily soul and body. I live without God in the world, and shall die miserably." Mr. F.D. with whom he had not been in habits of business offered, to join him in an Adventure. It succeeded far beyond their expectation. Mr. F.D. said when they wound it up, "one thing you know, I have been long in business, began with very little—have built a house, and have enough to build another. I have generally succeeded in undertakings and attribute all to this or that whether they are great or small, I always ask a blessing of God, and look to that blessing for success." William says "I was struck with shame and sorrow that I had been as a heathen before God." These he called his two warnings which awakened his soul. He speaks of them always with tears.

O the promises he makes, if it pleases God to spare him. We have had one Mate to see us from Captain O'Brien; talked out of the window to him. Also one of the Sailors who seemed to love us like his own soul always flying to serve, and trying to please us while on board came with him. Poor Charles, he turned pale when he saw my head out of the iron bars and called out "Why, dear Mrs. Seton, are you in a prison?" He looked behind

---

[40] Matthew 16:26.

all the way as he went shaking his head at Anna as long as he could see her. Charles had lived at the quarantine at Staten Island and that, [even] without his good and affectionate heart, would make me love him. I shall never hear a sailor's "Yo! Yo!" without thinking of his melancholy song. He is the captain's and everybody's favorite.

How gracious is my Adored Master who gives even to the countenance of the stranger the look of kindness and pity. From the time we first landed here, one of the guards of our room looked always with sorrow and sympathy on us and although I cannot understand him, nor he me, we talk away very fast. He showed me yesterday that he was very sick by pointing to his breast and throat. When the Capitano came, I told him how sorry I was for poor Filippo. "Oh, Signora, he is very well off. He has been two years married to a very, very beautiful girl of 16—has two children, and receives 3/6 per day[41]—to be sure he is obliged to sleep in the Lazaretto but in the morning goes home to his wife for an hour or two. It is not possible to spare him longer from his duty et que voulez-vous, Signora."

Good and Merciful Father, Who gives content and a cheerful heart. With 3/6 per day, a wife and children to maintain with such a pittance. Often let me think of Filippo when I have not enough, or think I have not. He is 22; his wife 18—thought goes to two children at home—most dear B and H—[42]

Went to the railings with little Anna to receive from our Capitano's daughter a baby doll she had been making for her. She has a kind, good countenance and hangs on her Father's arm. She has refused an offer of marriage that she may take care of him. Such a sight awakened many recollections. I hope she may meet the one she loves, who will reward her.

1st December 1803

Arose between 6 and 7, before the day had dawned, the light of the moon opposite our window was still strongest—not a breath of wind—the sea which before I had always seen in violent commotion now gently seemed to creep to the rocks it had so long been beating over—everything around at rest except two little white gulls flying to the westward towards my home—towards my loves—that thought did not do—flying towards

---

[41] The daily wage of a prison guard.

[42] Elizabeth was reminded of her half-brother Barclay (Andrew Barclay Bayley) and Harriet Seton, a sister-in-law, who were planning to marry.

Heaven—where I tried to send my soul—the Angel of Peace met it and poured over the oil of love and praise, driving off every vain imagination and led it to its Saviour and its God. "We Praise Thee, O God!"—the dear strain of praise in which I always seem to meet the souls I love and "Our Father." These two portions are the union of love and praise and in them I meet the Soul of my Soul. At ten o'clock read with Will and Anna—at twelve he was at rest—Anna playing in the next room. Alone to all the world, one of those sweet pauses in spirit when the body seems to be forgotten, came over me.

In the year 1789 when my Father was in England[43] I jumped in the wagon that was driving to the woods for brush about a mile from Home. The boy who drove it began to cut brush and I set off in the woods where I soon found an outlet in a meadow and a chestnut tree, with several young ones growing round it, attracted my attention as a seat, but when I came to it, I found rich moss under it and a warm sun. Here then was a sweet bed. The air still—a clear blue vault above, the numberless sounds of spring melody and joy—the sweet clover and wild flowers I had gotten by the way, and a heart as innocent as a human heart could be was filled with even enthusiastic love to God and admiration of His Works. Still I can feel every sensation that passed through my soul. I thought at that time that my Father did not care for me. Well, God was my Father—my All. I prayed, sang hymns, cried, laughed in talking to myself of how far He could place me above all sorrow. Then I laid still to enjoy the heavenly peace that came over my soul; and I am sure that in the two hours which I so enjoyed, that I grew ten years in my spiritual life. I told cousin Joe Bayley to go home with his wood, not to mind me and walked a mile round to see the roof of the parsonage, where lived the parson, of course. Then I made another hearty prayer—then sung all the way home—with a good appetite for the samp[44] and fat pork.

Well, all this came strong in my head this morning when, as I tell you the body let the Spirit alone. I had both prayed and cried heartily which is my daily and often hourly comfort. Closing my eyes, with my head on the table, lived all these sweet hours over again, making believe that I was under the chestnut tree. I felt so peaceable, a heart—so full of love to God—such confidence and hope in Him and made my hearty prayer not for the Son but The Parson himself, dwelling with delight on the hope of all meeting

[43] Dr. Richard Bayley studied medicine in London on several occasions.
[44] Samp is a type of porridge made from coarsely ground Indian corn.

again in unity of Spirit, in the Bond of Peace, and that Holiness which will be perfected in the Union Eternal—the wintry storms of time shall be over, and the unclouded spring enjoyed forever.

So, you see, as you know, with God for our portion there is no prison in high walls and bolts—no sorrow in the soul that waits on him though beset with present cares, and gloomy prospects. For this freedom I can never be sufficiently thankful, as in my William's case, it keeps alive what in his weak state of body would naturally fail. Often when he hears me repeat the Psalms of Triumph in God, and read Saint Paul's faith in Christ with my whole soul, it so enlivens his Spirit that he also makes them his own, and all our sorrows are turned into joy. Oh well, may I love God! Well may my whole soul strive to please Him, for what but the strain of an Angel can ever express what He has done and is constantly doing for me. While I live, while I have my being, in time and through Eternity, let me sing praises to my God.

2nd December

Enjoyed the morn, and daybreak—read the commentary on 104th Psalm,[45] and sang hymns in bed till 10—a hard frost in the night—endeavored to make a fire in my room with brush, but was smoked out—the poor strangers almost mad with hunger and cold, quarreled, battled—and at last sat down in companies on the grass with cards which made them as noisy as their anger—Patience—

Anna sick, William tired out—was obliged to say my dear Service by myself—a clear sunset which cheered my heart though it was all the while singing "from lowest depth of woe"—the Ave Maria bells ring while the sun sets, on one side of us and the bells "for the dead" on the other. The latter sometimes continue a long while. In the morning the bells always call again to prayer for the "Souls in Purgatory." Our Capitano said a good deal on the pleasure I should enjoy on Christmas at Pisa in seeing all their ceremonies. The enjoyment of Christmas—Heavenly Father who knows my inmost soul, He knows how it would enjoy—and will also pity while it is cut off from what it so much longs for. One thing is in my power, though communion with those my soul loves is not within my reach, in one sense, but in the other, what can deprive me of it, "still in Spirit we may meet." At 5 o'clock here, it will be 12 there—at 5, then in some quiet corner on my knees I may

---

[45] Ps. 104 appears as Ps. 105 in contemporary Catholic Bibles.

spend the time they are at the altar, and if the "cup of Salvation"[46] cannot be received in the strange land evidently, virtually it may, with the Blessing of Christ and the "cup of Thanksgiving" supply in a degree, that, which if I could obtain would be my strongest desire. Oh my soul, what can shut us out from the love of Him who will even dwell with us through love.

4th December[47]

Our Captain O'Brien and his wife found their way to us. "Must not touch Signora," says Filippo, the guard in the Lazaretto, dividing us with his stick—kind affectionate Captain when I ran down to meet him, the tears danced in his eyes, while poor Willy and Anna peeped through the grates. Mrs. O'Brien began to cry. We could not see them but a few minutes for the cold.

Our Lazaretto Captain has sent hand-irons, small wood, etc., and I have doctored the chimney with a curtain (a sheet) so as to make the smoke bearable. I have had an anxious day between Will and Anna. She was very ill for some hours. When the cause of her sufferings removed, we went on our knees together. Oh, may her dear soul long send forth such precious tears. Dear, dear Rebecca, how often have we nursed up the little fire at night together as I do now alone—alone recall the Word—my Bible, commentaries, and Kempis, all visible and in continual enjoyment. When I cannot get hours, I take minutes. Invisible, O the company is numberless. Sometimes I feel so assured that the Guardian Angel is immediately present that I look from my book and can hardly be persuaded that I was not touched.

"Poor soul!" John Henry Hobart would say. "She will lose her reason in that prison." More than that I sometimes feel that his Angel is near and undertake to converse with it, but the enjoyments only come when all is quiet and I have passed an hour or two with King David, the Prophet Isaiah or become spiritually elevated by some of the commentaries. These hours I often think I shall hereafter esteem the most precious of my life.

My Father and my God, who by the Consoling Voice of His Word builds up the soul in hope so as to free it even for hours of its encumbrance, confirming, and strengthening it by the constant experience of His Indulgent

---

46 Ps. 116:13.

47 Elizabeth Seton also included her experiences of December 4th in a previous letter. See 2.6, *Seton Collected Writings*, 1:250.

Goodness—giving it a new life in Him even while in the midst of pains and sorrows—sustaining, directing, consoling and blessing through every changing scene of its pilgrimage, making His Will its guide to temporal comfort and eternal glory. How shall the most unwearied diligence, the most cheerful compliance, the most humble resignation ever be enough to express my love, my joy—thanksgiving and praise—

12th December

A week has past, my dear Sister, without even one little memorandum of the pen. The first day of it, that dear day in which I always find my blessing, was passed in interrupted prayers, anxiety, and watching.

Monday 5th was early awakened by my poor Will in great suffering. I sent for Doctor Tutilli, who as soon as he saw him told me—he was not wanted, but I must send for him who would minister to his soul. In this moment, I stood alone, as to this world. My husband looked in silent agony at me and I at him, each fearing to weaken the other's strength. At the moment he drew himself towards me and said, "I breathe out my soul to you." The exertion he made assisted nature's remaining force and he threw a quantity from his lungs, which had threatened to stop their motion, and in so doing experienced so great a revolution that in a few hours afterwards he seemed nearly the same as when we first entered the Lazaretto. Oh that day! It was spent close by his bedside on my little mat. He slumbered the most of every hour, and did I not pray and did I not praise God. No enquiring visitor disturbed the solemn silence, no breakfast nor dinner to interrupt the rest. Guy Carleton came at sunset. They thought Mrs. Filicchi was dying—he thought his poor brother-in-law so—Then came our Capitano with so much offered kindness. He was shocked at the tranquility of my poor Will and distressed at the thought that I was alone with him for the doctor had told him that notwithstanding his present relief, if the expectoration from the lungs did not return, he might be gone in a few hours. Would I have someone in the room? Oh no, what had I to fear? What had I to fear? I laid down, as if to rest, that Will might not be uneasy but listened all night—sometimes by the fire, sometimes lying down—sometimes I thought his breathing stopped—and kissed his poor face to feel if it was cold—and sometimes alarmed by its heaviness—well—was I alone? Dear indulgent Father, could I be alone while clinging fast to Thee in continued prayer or thanksgiving? Prayer for him, and joy, wonder, and delight to feel assured that what I had so fondly hoped and confidently asserted really proved in the hour of trial to be more than I could hope, more than I could conceive—that my God could and would bear me through even the most severe trials with that strength, confidence, and trust, which if every circumstance of the case was considered, seemed more than a human being could expect or hope—but His Consolations—who shall speak them? How can utterance be given to that which only His Spirit can feel?

At daylight the wished for change took place. Mr. Hall[48] came in the morning with Mr. Filicchi and the Capitano. He went away with a promise to come again. The intervening days and evenings have been spent in constant attention to the *main-concern* but from a singularity of disposition which rather delights in going on, than in retrospecting sorrow, have rather (when I could only keep awake by writing according to the old custom) busied myself in writing the first sermon for my dear little Dick.

Will goes on gently, but keeps me busy. Anna is a treasure. She was reading yesterday that John was imprisoned.[49] "Yes, Papa, Herod imprisoned him and Miss Herodias gave him liberty." I clarified, "No, my dear, she had him beheaded!" "Well, Papa, she released him from prison and sent him to God." Child after my own heart!

Tuesday 13th

Five days more and our quarantine is ended. Lodgings are engaged at Pisa on the borders of the Arno River.[50] My heart used to be very full of poetical visions about this famous river, but it has no room for visions now. One only vision is before it. No one ever saw my Willy without giving him the quality of an amiable man, but to see that character exalted to the peaceful, humble Christian, waiting the Will of God with a patience that seems more than human, and a firm faith which would do honor to the most distinguished! Piety, is a happiness allowed only to the poor little Mother who is separated from all other happiness that is connected with this scene of things. No sufferings, nor weakness nor distress (and from these, he is never free in any degree) can prevent his following me daily in prayer, portions of the Psalms, and generally large portions of the Scriptures. If he is a little better, he enlarges his attention, if worse, he is the more eager not to lose a moment. Except the day which we thought might be his last, he has never failed one day in this course, since our entrance into these stone walls

[48] Rev. Thomas Hall was the Protestant chaplain to the British consulate in Livorno.
[49] Matthew 14:3-12.
[50] The Filicchi family arranged lodging in Pisa, about fifteen miles from Livorno.

the 19th November. He very often says this is the period of his life which, if he lives or dies, he will always consider as blessed—the only time which he has not lost—not the smallest murmur. Oh! Lifting up of the eyes, is the strongest expression I have yet heard from him in the rapid progress of his complaint which has reduced him to almost nothing. From its very nature gives him no release from irritation in violent coughing, chills, oppressions, weakness and even in the weight of his own limbs seems more than a mortal could bear. "Why art thou so heavy, O my Soul," is the only comfort he seems to find in words. He often talks of his darlings—but most of meeting, ONE family in Heaven; talks of those we have left behind as if it was not yesterday, and of dear Henry Hobart whose visits and society he misses most, as they would be his greatest consolation in these hours of sorrow.

When I thank God for my "creation and preservation" it is with a warmth of feeling I never could know until now—to wait on him my Will *soul and body*—to console and soothe those hours of affliction and pain, weariness and watching, which next to God, I alone could do—to strike up the cheerful notes of hope and Christian triumph, which from his partial love, he hears with the more enjoyment from me because, to me, he attributes the greatest share of them. To hear him in pronouncing the name of his Redeemer and declare that I first taught him the sweetness of the sound—Oh, if I was in the dungeon of this Lazaretto, I should bless and praise my God for these days of retirement and abstraction from the world which have afforded leisure and opportunity for so blessed a work.

14th Said my prayers alone while Will was asleep. I did not dare remind him of them for weakness and pain quite overpower him. Rain and storm, as indeed we have had almost every day of the 26 we have been here. The dampness about us would be thought dangerous for a person in health, and my Will's sufferings—Oh! well I know that God is above. Capitano, you need not always point your silent look and finger there. If I thought our condition the providence of man, instead of the "weeping Magdalene"[51] as you so graciously call me, you would find me a lioness willing to burn your Lazaretto about your ears, if it were possible that I might carry off my poor prisoner to breathe the air of Heaven in some more seasonable place. To keep a poor soul who came to your country for his life, thirty days shut up in damp walls, smoke, and wind from all corners blowing, even the curtain round his bed, which is only a mattress on boards and his bones almost

---
[51] Cf. John 20:13.

through—and now the shadow of death, trembling if he only stands a few minutes. He is to go to Pisa for his health. This day his prospects are very far from Pisa.

O my Heavenly Father, I know that these contradictory events are permitted and guided by Thy Wisdom, which only is light. We are in darkness, and must be thankful that our knowledge is not wanted to perfect Thy Work—and also keep in mind that infinite Mercy which in permitting the sufferings of the perishing body has provided for our souls so large an opportunity of comfort and nourishment for our Eternal Life, where we shall assuredly find that all things have worked together for our good—for our sure trust in Thee.

Thursday. Finished reading the New Testament through, which we began the 6th October and my Bible as far as Ezekiel, which I have always read to myself in rotation, but the lessons appointed in the Prayer Book, to Will—today read him several passages in Isaiah, which he enjoyed so much that he was carried for awhile beyond his troubles. Indeed our reading is an unfailing comfort. Will says he feels like a person brought to the Light after many years of darkness when he heard the Scriptures as the law of God and therefore Sacred, but not discerning what part he had in them or feeling that they were the Fountain of Eternal Life.

Friday night—A heavy day, part of our service together—part alone. They have bolted us in tonight, expecting to find my Will gone tomorrow—but he rests quietly—and God is with us.

Saturday and Sunday—Melancholy days of combat with nature's weakness, and the courage of hope which pictured our removal from the Lazaretto to Pisa.

Monday morning—Arose with the light and had everything prepared for the anxious hour. At ten, all in readiness and at eleven held the hand of my Will while he was seated on the arms of two men and conducted from the Lazaretto to Filicchi's coach, surrounded by a multitude of gazers, all sighing out "O Pauverino"[52] while my heart beat almost to fainting, least he would die in the exertion. The air revived him, his spirit was cheerful, and through fifteen miles of heavy roads, he was supported, and appeared stronger than when he set out. My Father and my God! was all my full heart of thankfulness could utter.

---

[52] "O poor man!"

Tuesday, 20th December—Let me stop and ask myself if I can go through the remainder of my memorandum with that sincerity and exactness which has so far been adhered to. Whether in the crowd of anxieties and sorrows, which are pressed in so small a compass of time, the overflowing of feeling can be suppressed and my soul stand singly before my God—yes—every moment of it speaks his praise and therefore it shall be followed.

Tuesday, 20th December—My Seton was composed the greater part of the day on a sofa delighted with his change of situation, taste, and elegance, of everything around him, having every necessary comfort within his reach. We read, compared past and present, talked of heavenly hopes, and with our dear Guy Carleton, (who was to stay with us four days), and then went to rest in hopes of a good night. I had scarcely fixed the pillows of the sofa on which I made my bed before Will called me to help him, and from that moment the last complaint (of the bowels) which Dr. Tutilli told me must be decisive, came on.

Wednesday—A kind of languid weakness seized the mind as well as overpowered the body, he must and would ride. The physician Dr. Cartelatch whispered to me that he might die in the attempt, but there was no possibility of refusal and it was concluded that opposition was worse than any risk. He was carried down in a chair, and supported in my trembling arms with pillows—we rode—Oh, my Father, well did you strengthen me in that struggle! In five minutes we were forced to return, and to get him out of the coach, into the chair, up the stairs, and on the bed. Words can never tell!

Thursday—A cloudy day, and quiet—

Friday—The complaint seemed lessened and ride again we must. We took Madame de Tot, (the lady of the house) with us. He returned in better spirits and more able to help himself than when we went out, and I really began to think that riding must be good—but that was the last.

Saturday—Constant suffering and for the first day he was confined in bed. The disorder of the bowels was so violent that he said he could not last till morning. Yet he talked with cheerfulness about his darlings and thanked God with great earnestness that he had given him so much time to reflect, and such consolation in His Word, and prayer. With the help of a small portion of Laudanum,[53] he rested until midnight. He then awoke, and

---

[53] A type of sedative.

observed I had not laid down. I said, "No, Love, for the sweetest reflections keep me awake—Christmas day is begun—the day of our dear Redeemer's birth here. You know this is the day that opened to us the door of Everlasting Life." "Yes." he said, "and how I wish we could have the Sacrament."[54] Well we must do all we can. Putting a little wine in a glass, I said different portions of Psalms and prayers which I had marked, hoping for a happy moment. We took the Cup of Thanksgiving, setting aside the sorrow of time, in the views of the joys of Eternity. Oh! So happy to find that those joys were more strongly painted to him. On Sunday, O'Brien came, and my Will gave me in his charge to take me home with a composure and solemnity, that made us cold. I did not pass a mouthful through my lips that day, which was spent on my knees by his bedside. Every moment I could look off of my Will, he anxiously prayed to be released that day, and followed me in prayer whenever he had the least cessation from extreme suffering.

Monday—Was so impatient to be gone that I could scarcely persuade him to wet his lips, but continued calling his Redeemer to pardon and release him. He always would have the door of his room shut, so I had no interruption. Guy Carleton kept Anna out of the way, and every promise in the Scriptures I could remember and suitable prayer, I continually repeated to him, which seemed to be his only relief. When I stopped to give anything, "Why do you do it? What do I want? I want to be in Heaven. Pray, pray, for my Soul." He said he felt so comfortable an assurance that his Redeemer would receive him, that he saw his dear little Tat smiling before him, and told Anna "Oh, if Papa could take you with him," and at midnight when the cold sweat came on would reach out both his arms to me, and said repeatedly "you promised me you would go, come, come, fly."

At four the hard struggle ceased, nature sunk into a settled sob, "My dear Wife, and little ones!" and "My Christ Jesus, have mercy and receive me!" was all I could distinguish and again repeated "My Christ Jesus!" until a quarter past seven, when the dear soul took its flight to the Blessed Exchange it so much longed for.

I often asked him when he could not speak, "You feel, my love, that you are going to your Redeemer?" He motioned, "Yes," with a look up of peace. At a quarter past 7 on Tuesday morning 27th December, his soul was released, and mine from a struggle next to death.

---

[54] Holy Communion.

And how will my dear Sister understand except if you could conceive the scene of suffering my William passed through. I took my little Anna in my arms and made her kneel with me again by the dear body, and thank our Heavenly Father for relieving him from his misery, for the joyful assurance that through our Blessed Redeemer, he had entered into Life Eternal and implored his protecting care and pity for us, who have yet to finish our course.

Now opening the door to let the people know it was finished—servants and the landlady all were at a loss about what should be done. Finding every one afraid of catching the complaint, as we should be of the yellow fever, I took two women who had washed and sometimes assisted me, and again shutting the door, with their assistance did the last duties. Felt I had done all—all that tenderest love and duty could do. My head had not rested for a week—three days and nights the fatigue had been incessant, and one meal in 24 hours. Still I must wash, dress, pack up, and in one hour be in Mrs. Filicchi's carriage and ride fifteen miles to Leghorn. Guy Carleton and our good old Louie stayed to watch and my Will was brought in the afternoon and deposited in the house [morgue] appointed in the Protestant burying ground.[55]

Oh! Oh! Oh! What a day! Close his eyes, lay him out, ride a journey, be obliged to see a dozen people in my room until night. Then at night crowded with the whole sense of my situation—O MY FATHER, and MY God! The next morning at eleven, all the English and Americans in Leghorn met at the grave house [morgue] and all was done.

In all this is it not necessary to dwell on the Mercy and Consoling Presence of my Dear Redeemer, for no mortal strength could support what I experienced.

My William often asked me if I felt assured that he would be accepted and pardoned, and I always tried to convince him that where the soul was so humble and sincere as his, and submission to God's Will so uniform as his had been throughout his trial, that it became sinful to doubt one moment of his reception through the merits of his Redeemer. The night before his death, I was praying earnestly for him that his pardon might be sealed in Heaven and his transgressions blotted out. After praying, I continued on my knees and leaned my head on the chair by which I knelt and insensibly

[55] The English burying ground at Saint John's Anglican Church in Livorno.

lost myself. I saw in my slumber a little angel with a pen in one hand and a sheet of pure white paper in the other. He looked at me holding out the paper and wrote in large letters JESUS. This though a vision of sleep, was a great comfort and he was very much affected when I told him. He said a few hours before he died, "the angel wrote JESUS—He has opened the Door of Eternal Life for me and will cover me with His Righteousness."

I had a similar dream the same night. The heavens appeared a very bright blue—a little angel at some distance held open a division in the sky—a large Black Bird like an Eagle flew towards me and flapped its wings round, and made everything dark. The angel looked as if it held up the division, waiting for something the bird came for. So alone from every friend on earth, walking the valley of the shadow of death,[56] we had sweet comfort even in our dreams—while faith convinced us that they were realities.

Leghorn, January 3rd 1804[57]

My own dearest Rebecca—

I have been looking over the long history of our voyage of which I had written you a faithful account to the last day of the past year, and as it is probable that Captain O'Brien will sail in a fortnight and I may be with you before this opportunity reaches Boston, and my letters yet get from Boston to you. I think, it best to take it to you myself, or if it is God's will that I do not see you, would not wish that the melancholy scenes of sorrow I have passed through should come to your knowledge, as you will all feel enough at hearing that our dear William is gone—gone stretching out his arms to his Saviour, and rejoicing at the moment of his release—

Our passage here was as comfortable as we could expect, and his prospects of recovery I think almost the same as when we left home, but thirty days passed in the Lazaretto, on the sea shore, exposed to a succession of heavy storms very unusual to this climate, and a large room always cold and full of smoke, added to confinement, and the regulations of not suffering even a physician to feel his pulse, (for whoever touched, or came within some yards of us, was subject to the same quarantine), all added, was more than he could bear, and eventually after having been many nights

---

[56] Ps. 23:4.
[57] 2.8, *Seton Collected Writings*, 1:276.

bolted in quarantine, with the assurance that he would die before morning, he was carried out and put in a coach which took us *to Pisa* a ride of fifteen miles, which, with pillows, cordials, etc., he bore much better than we expected. Two days before Christmas, he was taken to his bed with the last symptom of his disorder, a lax,[58] and from that day, everything he took passed immediately through him and I had to do for him as for a baby—he suffered at times, but was generally composed and so desirous of going to God that every nourishment I gave him, he would say: "I do not want that, I want to be in heaven," and found no comfort but in having his room always shut, and me on my knees by his bed side, night and day, to help him in his prayers.

Christmas Day he continually reminded himself "this day my Redeemer took pain and sorrow that I might have Peace; this day he gained eternal life for me"—and hoped so much that he would be called by God on that day—but Monday night about twelve the cold sweat began. He bid me carry the candle out of the room and shut the door, I did so—and remained on my knees holding his hand and praying for him till a quarter past seven, when his dear soul separated gently without any groan or struggle—I heard him repeatedly follow my prayers, and when I ceased a moment, he continued saying "My Christ, Jesus have mercy!"—also "My dear wife, my little ones." He told me: "Tell all my dear friends not to weep for me that I die happy, and satisfied with the Almighty Will." After he was gone and dear little Anna had prayed with me by his side, I sent for Madame de Tot, the mistress of the house, but found that their terror of his complaint (which they looked at with as much dread as we do the Yellow Fever) was so great that I could expect no assistance from them, therefore I was obliged with the assistance of a poor woman who had washed for him, to lay him out myself, which added to three nights not laying my head down, and two days fasting seemed almost enough. Notwithstanding I was forced to ride the fifteen miles to Leghorn with Mrs. Filicchi without even lying down, as my dear William must be carried there to be buried, as it is a law that it must be done within the 24 hours.

However by putting him in the burying house in the church yard we were allowed to wait until eleven the next day, which allowed time to send notice to the Americans and English in the place. They all attended,

---

[58] A disorder of the bowels.

the consul,[59] and our clergyman (Rev. Hall), and every respect was shown according to his own directions which he gave me in the way of conversation with the greatest composure that I might not have any trouble by being in doubt of what was right. He also sent for Captain O'Brien and gave me in his charge in the most calm manner. He took a strange fancy in his mind that he had received a letter from the letter office in London telling him that my ticket, which he had renewed there, had drawn the Royal Prize and that James, his younger brother, had also written to him that he had not a single bill out in the world—this was the effect of extreme weakness and I never contradicted him in it, as it was a source of the greatest comfort and satisfaction to him. He thanked God always with so much earnestness that now he was not wanted by authorities for our support, he took him first that he might not see us die, and that while he was wanted, he was spared—O'Brien and Filicchi all agreed we must let him think accordingly.

Here I anxiously await, my dear Sister, for the day of sailing—the Filicchis do all they can to ease my situation and seem indeed that they cannot do enough—indeed from the day we left home, we have met with nothing but kindness even in the servants and strangers—Mrs. Mary Filicchi (Filippo's wife) has been in bed ever since our arrival until the day she came to fetch me from <u>Pisa,</u> and Antonio Filicchi, run down with business matters, did all he could for us and Guy Carleton, too, is all affection both to me and my Anna—

We have not heard one word from Home—O'Brien talks of going to Barcelona but as it is in the straits and on our way home, will make but a few days difference—Home—O my heavenly Father, shall I once more be <u>there</u>! My Seton said "when you are all again together, don't say, 'poor William,' for I shall be in heaven, and trust you will come to me, and make my darlings always look for me there." Oh how "good and gracious" has the Lord been in giving such consolation—What shall I say of love to all—an ocean of love would not be enough—to my dear girls, my darling, my dear Eliza my all————

Tell my dear friend John Henry Hobart that I do not write because the opportunity is unexpected and my breast is very weak after all its struggles—that I have a long letter I wrote on board of ship to him—that I am hard pushed by these charitable Roman Catholics who wish that so much goodness should be improved by a conversion (to their faith), which

---

[59] Thomas Appleton.

to effect they have even taken the trouble to bring me their best informed Priest, Father Peter Plunkett, who is an Irishman. They find me so willing to hear their enlightened conversation, that consequently as learned people like to hear themselves, best, I have but little to say, and as yet keep friends with all as the best comment on my religious profession—

My William said he saw his <u>Tate</u> while he was dying—is she too in heaven? Thy will be done! How do I know how many are gone? Thy will be done—<u>It is my Father's</u>. I think I may hope to be with you on Ash Wednesday if I do not mistake the day, coming in April—not within God's house (<u>but in Spirit</u>) since I left you, and the 27ᵗʰ December the first night I have taken off my clothes to sleep since the 4ᵗʰ of October—always watching—I shall write also to my dear sister, Mary Post, and to everyone else, my girls, Andrew Barclay Bayley, my Joseph Bayley, etc., you must explain to them that I cannot write—I write so small because it is to go by post—which I believe will be very high.

To all the family and to Phoebe, Mary, Mammy, Dina Sur, all remember me—tell James Seton that I have my William's journal as long as he could write, which I will bring to him—Remember me affectionately to William D. Seton and his wife—and her family—

Tell Aunt Elizabeth Farquhar—<u>read this letter to her</u>—that my William always talked of her and wished that she could know how happy he was—I wrote to her on board ship also to tell her how he was—also to Eliza Sadler—all these I shall bring—If—My Soul has heavenly blessing, dearest Rebecca—"<u>The Protecting Presence and consoling grace of my Redeemer and God</u>" has never left me—

Your own, own Sister *EAS.*

Leghorn, 6ᵗʰ January 1804[60]

My own dearest Rebecca,

Two days ago I wrote you by way of Salem (Boston) and have since heard that there is a fast sailing vessel bound to Baltimore, and think it best to write by both opportunities—though I have nothing but melancholy and sorrow to communicate. In that letter, I have written you some of the particulars of my dear William's departure, death I cannot call it, where the

---

[60] 2.9, *Seton Collected Writings*, 1:280.

release is so happy as his was. It is my case that would be death to any one not supported by the Almighty Comforter, but his Mercy has supported, and still upholds, and in it alone I trust. I also wrote you that Captain O'Brien has appointed the 15th of this month for his day of sailing, but do not think it will be before the 20th, and instead of Ash Wednesday, which I thoughtlessly mentioned as the time I expect to be with you, I should have said the 1st of April, and shall bless God indeed if it is then. Once more to see my darlings seems to be more happiness than I dare to ask for. My William charged me always to make them look for him in heaven—and must you, my dearest Rebecca, first point it out to them—that they shall see their Father no more in this world.

I shall enclose this letter to Jack Curzon Seton,[61] and as it hurts me to write, will write only to you, as I have sent by the Salem vessel letters to my sister, Mrs. Sadler, Uncle John Charlton, John Wilkes,[62] and yourself I have not heard one word from America except by Captain Blagge of *The Pyomingo*, who said that business had recommenced and the inhabitants returned to New York early in November.[63]

My dear William's sufferings and death has interested so many persons here, that I am as kindly treated and as much attended to both as to my health and every consolation that they can offer to me, as if I was at home. Indeed, when I look forward to my unprovided situation as it relates to the affairs of this life, I must often smile at their tenderness and precautions—Anna says "O Mamma, how many friends God has provided for us in this strange land, for they are our friends before they know us." Who can tell how great a comfort he provided for me when he gave her to me. Richard Bayley is at Cadiz, a seaport in Spain, and I believe does not know of our being here as he has performed a long quarantine in consequence of is having been at Malaga[64] while the plague was there—

---

[61] John (Jack) Curzon Seton was a brother-in-law to Elizabeth Seton.

[62] Friend, business associate, and husband of Mary Seton Wilkes, a first cousin of William Magee Seton. As a young man, John Wilkes, had been helped by the elder William Seton. The Wilkes became friends of the younger Setons, and John Wilkes remained an adviser, confidante, and supporter of Elizabeth Seton after William Magee's death and her conversion, never forgetting her kindness during his wife's last illness.

[63] Yellow Fever had flared up in the summer of 1803 and many residents had fled New York City.

[64] A province in southern Spain.

Guy Carlton Bayley is as affectionate as possible—he was with us at Pisa when my William died, but could not be of any use but in keeping everybody away from his room as he [Will] could not have any one near him but me and even disliked to have the door opened—he was so anxious to keep his mind fixed on his approaching hour that when any one spoke it seemed as if he only felt pain and anxiety that they should be gone. Again, let me repeat, that in everything that related to his dear soul, I had every comfort that I could expect and the surest grounds of hope, through the merits of Our Redeemer—

When I say I send my love to you all, I send my whole heart, and could almost say my soul, only that it is not mine——

I have the prospect of still watching and care during my voyage, for our Captain's wife is in the family way and is often very ill—she was so ill New Year's night that I was obliged to go, before a carriage could be got, mud over shoes, and be hoisted up the ship to remain on board until the next day. She treated us sadly coming here, brought a baby with the whooping cough, also a servant boy who with the child's coughing and crying all day and most of the night, and the mother's scolding, was a great disturbance to my William. Finally poor Anna got it too and often hindered his getting rest—for me it is all alike—but these three months have been a hard lesson. Pray for me that I may make a good use of it—dear, dear, Rebecca, heaven bless you!

Your *EAS.*

If there could be any faith in singularly impressive and repeated dreams our dear John Henry Hobart is in heaven, too—how much William used to wish for him—My best love to his wife—

28th January 1804[65]

My Rebecca, My Soul's Sister–

How many new thoughts and affections pass my mind in a day, and you so far away to whom I would wish to tell all—after the last sorrowful word at Pisa where my Will died, what shall I say—arrived at Mr. Antonio Filicchi's home. He gave the look of many sympathies as he helped me from his carriage, and showed me to my chamber where his most amiable lady

[65] 2.11, *Seton Collected Writings*, 1:288.

and sweet Anna looked in my face as if to comfort, but my poor high heart was in the clouds roving after my William's soul and repeating, "My God, you are my God,[66] and so I am now alone in the world with You and my little ones, but you are my Father and doubly theirs." Mrs. Filicchi very tired with our ride left me to rest—

Evening. Then came Parson Thomas Hall—a kind man indeed— "as the tree falls, Mam—there it lies," was his first address to me—who was little mindful of his meaning then—our good old capitano[67] also came with a black crape on the hat and arm and such a look of sorrow at his poor Signora—all his kindness in the Lazaretto was present, dearest Anna melted his heart again—and he ours—so many tender marks of respect and compassion and boundless generosity from the two families of Filicchis— the first night of rest with little Anna's tender doting heart alone—the first night of rest since October 2nd—and long, long before that—as you well know—

"Saint Francis de Sales Day" (said Mr. Filippo Filicchi, as he entered our room) "I will give you a copy of his *Devout Life*[68] to amuse you"—amuse it truly did—how many times I was on my knees from strong impression of its powerful persuasion begging our God to make me so and so, as he said.

Silence and peace enough in our chamber—Anna would say as the different enquiries would be made "Could they do anything for us? Why truly, Ma, everybody is our friend."

2nd February 1804

This is some particular festival here[69]—Mrs. F. took me with her to Mass as she calls it, and we say to church—I don't know how to say the awful effect at being where they told me God was present in the Blessed Sacrament, and the tall pale meek heavenly looking man[70] who did *I don't know what* for I was at the side of the altar, so that I could not look up without seeing his countenance on which many lights from the altar reflected, and gave such strange impressions to my soul that I could but cover my face with my hands and let the tears run—oh my, the very little while we were there will

---

[66] Ps. 63:1.

[67] The man who had guarded the Setons when they were in the San Jacopo Lazaretto in Livorno.

[68] Saint Francis de Sales is the author of *Introduction to the Devout Life*, a spiritual classic.

[69] The Feast of the Presentation of Jesus at the Temple has also been called the Feast of the Purification of the Virgin and is celebrated on February 2.

[70] The priest who was celebrating the Sacred Liturgy of the Eucharist (Mass).

never be forgotten, though I saw nothing and no one, but this more than human person as he seemed to me—

Now we go to Florence—Mr. and Mrs. Antonio Filicchi are positive [insistent]—ah me—but that is not the way my heart goes, for it is not towards America—but Captain O'Brien is to be ready by our return...

I have made my little journal to Florence separate for you, as you will see—and when we meet, I have so much to tell you about things you do not dream of—these dear people are so strange about religion...

Four days I have been at Florence, lodged in the famous Palace of Medicis,[72] which fronts the Arno River and prevents a view of the high mountains[73] covered with elegant country seats, and five bridges across the river which are always thronged with people and carriages.

On Sunday 8th January at eleven o'clock went with Mrs. Filicchi to the chapel, La SS. Annunziata—passing through a curtain, my eye was struck with hundreds of people kneeling, but the gloom of the chapel which is lighted only by the wax tapers on the altar and a small window at the top darkened with green silk, made every object at first appear indistinct, while that kind of soft and distant music which lifts the mind to a foretaste of heavenly pleasure called up in an instant every dear and tender idea of my soul, and forgetting Mrs. Filicchi, companions, and all the surrounding scene. I sunk to my knees in the first place I found vacant, and shed a torrent of tears at the recollection of how long I had been a stranger in the house of my God, and the accumulated sorrow that had separated me from it. I need not tell you that I said our dear Service with my whole soul, as far as in its agitation, I could recollect. When the organ ceased and Mass was over, we walked round the Chapel, the elegance of ceilings in carved gold, altar loaded with gold, silver, and other precious ornaments, pictures of every sacred subject and the dome a continued representation of different parts of Scripture—all this can never be conceived by description—nor my delight in seeing old men and women, young women, and all sorts of

---

[71] 2.10, *Seton Collected Writings*, 1:283. Internal evidence indicates that Elizabeth wrote this entry in early February at Florence.

[72] Palazzo Medici Riccardi.

[73] The Tuscan Apennine Mountains dot the horizon of Tuscany.

people kneeling promiscuously about the altar as inattentive to us, or any other passengers, as if we were not there. On the other side of the Church, another Chapel presented a similar scene, but as another Mass had begun, I passed tip toe behind Mrs. Filicchi, unable to look round, though everyone is so intent on their prayers and Rosary, that it is very immaterial what a stranger does.

While Mrs. Filicchi went to make visits, I visited the Church of S. Firenze[74] and saw two more elegant chapels but in a more simple style and had the pleasure of treading the sacred place with two of its inhabitants, as a Convent is also part of the building. Saw a young priest unlock his little chapel with that composed and equal eye as if his soul had entered before him. My heart would willingly have followed after him. Here was to be the best music, but at night, and no female could be admitted.

Rode to the Queens gardens[75] where I saw elms and firs, with edges of yew and ivy in beautiful verdure and cultivated fields appearing like our advanced spring. Indeed it was not possible to look without thinking, or to think without my soul crying out for those it loves in heaven or in earth, therefore I was forced to close my eyes and lean against the carriage as if sleepy, which the mild softness of the air and warmth of the sun seemed easily to excuse.

Stopped at the Queen's Country Palace[76] and passed through such innumerable suites of apartments so elegant that each was a new object of wonder, but Solomon's vanity and vexation of spirit was all the while in my head.

Saw the Queen twice, but as little Anna says she would not be known from any other woman [except] but by the number of her attendants.

Sunday evening Mr. Trueman, Coffin, and Mrs. Filicchi went to the Opera.[77] I had a good fire in my room, locked the doors, and with my Anna, books, and pen passed a happy evening for this world. When we said our dear service together, Anna burst in to tears as she has always done since we say it alone. She says, "My dear Papa is praising God in Heaven, and I ought not to cry for him, but I believe it is human nature, is it not

---

[74] Church of San Firenze.
[75] Boboli Gardens.
[76] The Palazzo Pitti.
[77] The Opera House.

Mamma?" I think of what David said "I shall go to him, he cannot return to me." Her conversation is dearer to me and preferable to any I can have this side of the grave—it is one of the greatest mercies that I was permitted to bring her for many reasons.

Monday morning visited the Uffizi Gallery[78] but as my curiosity had been greatly excited by my Seton's descriptions, and the French have made great depredations, it did not equal my expectations. The chief d'oeuvre of Donatello—a head scarcely to be distinguished from life, the Redeemer about 12 years of age—a Madonna holding an hour glass in one hand and a skull in the other with a smiling look expressing, I fear neither time nor death. Madam Le Brun,[79] a French painter, and [the John] the Baptist very young were those that attracted me most. The statues in bronze were beautiful, but being only an American could not look very straight at them.[80]

Innumerable curiosities and antiquities surrounded on all sides. The Sacred representations were sufficient to engage and interest all my attention, and as the French had not been covetous of those, I had the advantage of my companions, but felt the void of him who would have pointed out the beauties of every object, too much to enjoy any perfectly. "Alone but half enjoyed." O My God!

Went to the Church of San Lorenzo where a sensation of delight struck me so forcibly that as I approached the great altar formed of all the most precious stones, marble, etc., that could be produced "My Soul does magnify the Lord, my spirit rejoices in God my Saviour" came into my mind with a fervor which absorbed every other feeling. It recalled the ideas of the offerings of David and Solomon to the Lord when the rich and valuable production of nature and art were devoted to his Holy Temple, and sanctified to his service. Annexed to this is the chapel of marble, the beauty and work, and richness of which might be supposed the production of more than mortal means, if its unfinished dome did not discover its imperfection. It is the Tomb of the Medicis[81] family, monuments of granite and lapis, golden crowns set with precious stones, the polish of the whole which reflects the different monuments as a mirror and the awful black Cosmos who are represented on the top of the monuments as large as life

---

[78] The Uffizi Art Gallery and Academy of Sculptors (Galleria dell'Accademia).
[79] Madame Elisabeth Vigée Lebrun (1755-1842) was a French neo-classical painter.
[80] American art did not yet depict the nude human body.
[81] The Capelle Medici is adjacent to the Church of San Lorenzo.

with their crowns and scepters, made my poor weak head turn. I believe if it had been possible that I should have been *alone* there, I would never have turned back again.

Passed my evening again in my room with dear Anna—at half past nine Mr. Coffin took the trouble to come for me from the Opera that I might hear some wonderful trio, in which the celebrated David[82] was to show all his excellence. As it would be over at ten, and Mrs. Filicchi so much desired it, I went with hat and veil, instead of the masks which they all wear. The Opera house is so dark that you scarcely can distinguish the person next to you. Anna thought the singers would go mad, and I could not find the least gratification in their quavers, felt the full conviction that those who could find pleasure in such a scene must be unacquainted with real pleasure. My William had so much desired that I should hear this David that I tried to be pleased, but not one note touched my heart. At ten I was released from the most unwilling exertion I had yet made, and returned with redoubled delight to my pleasures, which were as the joys of heaven in comparison.

Tuesday saw the Church of Sta. Maria Novella and the Queen's Palace in which she resides. Every beauty that gold, damask of every variety, and India tapestry can devise, embellished with fine statues, ceilings embossed with gold, elegant pictures, carpets and floors inlaid with the most costly satin woods in beautiful patterns, tables inlaid with most precious orders of stone, etc., all combine to make the Palace of Pitti[83] a pattern of elegance and taste, so say the connoisseur. For me, I am no Judge, as Ombrosi says.

A picture of the *Descent from the Cross* nearly as large as life engaged my whole soul. Mary at the foot of it expressed well that the iron had entered into her, and the shades of death over her agonized countenance so strongly contrasted the heavenly peace of the dear Redeemer's that it seems as if His pains had fallen on her. How hard it was to leave that picture and how often even in the few hours interval since I have seen it, I shut my eyes and recall it in imagination.

Abraham and Isaac also are represented in so expressive a manner that you feel the whole convulsion of the Patriarch's breast, and well for me that in viewing these two pictures [while] my companions were engaged

---

[82] Giacomo David was the most famous tenor of his time.
[83] The Palazzo Pitti.

with other subjects. The dropping tears could be hid, but the shaking of the whole frame not so easily. Dear Sister—H.H.—[if] you had your sigh in reflecting how truly you would enjoy them.[84]

Wednesday—This morning I have indeed enjoyed in The Anatomical Museum and Cabinet of Natural History—the "Work of the Almighty Hand" in every object. The anatomical rooms displaying nature in every division of the human frame is almost too much for human nature to support. Mine shrank from it, but recalling the idea of my God in all I saw, though so humiliating and painful in the view, still it was congenial to every feeling of my soul, and as my companion Trueman has an intelligent mind and an excellent heart, which for the time entered in to my feelings, I passed through most of the rooms uninterrupted in the sacred reflections they inspired. One of the rooms a female cannot enter...—and passed the door to the Cabinet of Natural History. The pleasures to be there enjoyed would require the attention of at least a month. In the short time I was allowed, I received more than I could have obtained in years, out of my own cabinet of precious things.

If I was allowed to choose an enjoyment from the whole theatre of human nature, it would be to go over those two hours again with my dear Brother Post [as] my companion...

Visited the Gardens called Boboli belonging to the Queen's Residence—Was well exercised in running up flights of steps in the style of hanging gardens and sufficiently repaid by the view of the environs of Florence, and the many varieties of beautiful evergreens with which this country abounds, and prevent the possibility of recollecting it is winter, except the cold and damp of their buildings, remind you of it. If the Tuscans are to be judged by their taste, they are a happy people, for everything without is very shabby, and within elegant. The exterior of their best buildings are to outward appearance in a state of ruin. Also saw the Academy of Sculpture[85] and the Garden of Simpla, and Botanical Garden[86]—O O O Heaven!!!!!

[84] Elizabeth Seton refers to the painting of Abraham and Isaac in the Church of Sta. Maria Novella.

[85] Galleria dell'Accademia.

[86] Giardini dei Simplici (Botanical Garden of San Marco).

10th February[87]

Well, my dearest, here is your Soul's Sister and little Anna truly in the joyful moment—we are to sail in a few days now...I asked Mr. Filippo Filicchi something (I don't know what) about the differences among religions and he began to tell me there was only one true religion, and without a right faith, we would not be acceptable to God—"O my Sir!" than said I, "If there is but one faith and nobody pleases God without it, where are all the good people who die out of it?" "I don't know," he answered, "That depends on what light of faith they had received, but I know where people will go who can know the right faith, if they pray for it and inquire for it, and yet do neither." Much as to say. "Sir you want me to pray and inquire and be of your faith?" said I laughing. "Pray and inquire," said he, "that is all I ask you."

So, dearest Bec, I am laughing with God when I try to be serious and say daily as the good gentleman told me in the poet Alexander Pope's words, "if I am right, O teach my heart still in the right to stay, if I am wrong Thy Grace impart to find the better way." Not that I can think there is a better way than I know—but everyone must be respected in their own beliefs. The other day a young Englishman brought the blood from my very heart to my face in the church of Montenero[88] where the Filicchi families took Anna and me to a lovely part of the country where Filippo Filicchi had been concealed by the blessed inhabitants of the monastery during some political revolution. They invited us to hear mass in their chapel. There this poor young Englishman at the very moment the Priest was doing the most sacred action they call the Elevation, (after the bread, you know, is blessed with the prayers, as they do when we go to communion)—just at that moment, this wild young man said loudly in my ear "this is what they call their REAL PRESENCE"—my very heart trembled with shame and sorrow for his unfeeling interruption of their sacred adoration, for all around was dead silence and many were prostrated. Involuntarily I bent from him to the pavement and thought secretly on the words of Saint Paul with starting tears "they discern not the Lords body."[89] My next thought was how should they eat and drink their very damnation for not discerning it, if indeed, it is

---

[87] 2.11, *Seton Collected Writings*, 1:290.

[88] The Shrine of Our Lady of Grace at Montenero is considered to be the site of many miraculous cures attributed to its painting of Our Lady of Montenero.

[89] 1 Cor. 11:17-34.

not there—yet how should it be there? How did He breathe my Soul in me, and how and how, a hundred other things, I know nothing about.

I am a Mother so the Mother's thought came also, how was my GOD a little babe in the first stage of his mortal existence in Mary, but I lost these thoughts in my babes at home, which I daily long for more and more, but they wait a fair wind—

18th February

Oh my God—GOD TRULY MINE or what would become of me— how can I tell you, Rebecca, my soul's Rebecca, how long before we meet? We were safe on board the vessel ready to sail the next morning, had parted with our most kind friends, loaded with their blessings and presents—I with gold and passports and recommendations, for fear of Algerians, or necessity to put in any of the Mediterranean ports[90]—but all that in vain—a driving storm at night struck the vessel against another boat, and in the morning instead of hoisting sail for America, we were obliged to return and go on shore—most kindly indeed welcomed by the Filicchis, but heart down enough at the disappointment. Imagine the rest when our sweetest Anna, unable to hide her suffering, was found in high fever. She was covered with eruptions which the doctor pronounced scarlettina[91]—O My—the darling tried to conceal all she could, but little guessed the whole consequence, for the doctor said the next day that I must give up the voyage—or the life of the child. Could you believe I was firm in choosing the latter, that is, in trusting her life and my hard case to our God since there was no other vessel for America in port—but Captain O'Brien came only to say that if he took us, he could not get a bill of health for Barcelona where he was forced to leave part of his cargo and a quarantine there would ruin his voyage.

The good man may have made this more evident because from my entrance in the ship the second time a most painful circumstance had taken place through my ignorance, and I was likely to have had a truly unhappy voyage, but what of that if I would, at the end of it, hold you and my darlings to my heart.

Well the hand of our God is all I must see in the whole—but it pinches to the Soul.

---

[90] Pirates were active in the Mediterranean at the time.
[91] Scarlettina is a version of scarlet fever.

24th—Close work with little Anna—she is over the worst though with such care and attention of everybody as would melt your heart. My very soul seems to be in her, sitting or laying all day and night by her side, in this strange but beautiful land—

My Sister dear, how happy would we be if we believed what these dear souls believe, that they possess God in the Sacrament and that He remains in their churches and is carried to them when they are sick, oh my! When they carry the Blessed Sacrament under my window while I feel the full loneliness and sadness of my case, I cannot stop the tears at the thought: my God how happy would I be even so far away from all so dear, if I could find You in the church as they do (for there is a chapel in the very house of Mr. Filicchi). How many things I would say to you of the sorrows of my heart and the sins of my life. The other day in a moment of excessive distress, I fell on my knees without thinking when the Blessed Sacrament[92] passed by and cried in an agony to God to bless me if He was there, that my whole Soul desired only Him. A little prayer book of Mrs. Filicchi's was on the table and I opened it to a little prayer (the *Memorare*) of Saint Bernard to the Blessed Virgin, begging her to be our Mother. I said it to her with such a certainty that God would surely refuse nothing to his Mother, and that she could not help loving and pitying the poor souls he died for. I felt really I had a Mother which you know my foolish heart so often lamented to have lost in my early days.[93] From the first remembrance of infancy, I have looked in all the plays of childhood and wildness of youth to the clouds for my Mother, and at that moment it seemed as if I had found more than her, even in tenderness and pity of a Mother—so I cried myself to sleep in her heart.

Leghorn, 5th March 1804[94]

My dearest Rebecca, must be very anxious for letters from her own Sister after that which Antonio Filicchi wrote John Wilkes by *The Shepherdess*. It pleases God to try me very hard in many ways—but also to bestow such favors and comforts that it would be worse than disobedience not to dwell on His Mercy, while I must bow to His dispensations. We were embarked

---

[92] Holy Eucharist.
[93] Elizabeth was not yet three years old when her mother died.
[94] 2.12, *Seton Collected Writings*, 1:293.

on board *The Shepherdess* and to sail the next morning but a storm driving back those vessels which had sailed before us, O'Brien could not venture out and while he waited a fair wind, my dear Anna was seized with violent fever and sore throat which proved to be the Scarlettina, and O'Brien was forced to leave me to my fate. She was eighteen days in bed, and the day she left it, I was obliged to go to mine with the same complaint. I have this day been a fortnight, not in great suffering, for I was too weak to receive any complaint violently, but suffered almost as much with that as I could have done other ways.

We came from being on board of ship to Antonio Filicchi's house and have received more than friendship—the most tender affection could not bestow more, and to crown all his goodness to me he has taken my passage in *The Pyomingo* with Captain Blagge who sails directly for New York as soon as the equinox is past. Antonio Filicchi accompanies us himself, as business and a wish to be acquainted with our country has long made the voyage necessary to him, and now the desire of restoring his "dear Sister" to her children and those she loves best, decides him to leave his dear little wife and children. He says this is due to all my dear Seton's love and friendship for him. Is it possible I have again the hope of seeing you so soon?

My God will do all—dear, dear Rebecca, to tell you what He has done for me though my bitter afflictions will require many, many happy evenings, which if He has in store for us, we will enjoy with thankful hearts, if not ____ I write only to you, and while I have been writing this feel so ill at my ease that I scarcely know how to go on—my whole heart, head, all are sick—but I think if I could once more be with you I should be well as ever.

Anna is very well and considered little less than an angel here. She has not improved in acquirements of general education, but in understanding and temper. The five months past are to her more than years. Once more shall I hold my dear ones in my arms! Heavenly Father, what an hour will that be! My dear fatherless children—fatherless to the world, but rich in God their Father for He will never leave us nor forsake us. I have been to my dear Seton's grave and wept plentifully over it with the unrestrained affection which the last sufferings of his life added to remembrance of former years, had made almost more than precious. When you read my daily memorandums since I left home, you will feel what my love has been, and acknowledge that God alone could support us through such proofs as has been required of it. Natural strength must have fallen the first trial—If it pleases God that we sail on *The Pyomingo*, and nothing extraordinary happens to lengthen our passage, I shall be with you nearly as soon as this, as our ship sails remarkably fast, and the season could not be more favorable.

Dear, dear Rebecca, the love I should send to all would be endless, therefore you must do all for me——

May God bless You dear Sister as He has blessed me, by blessing you with His Heavenly Consolations. Pray for me as I do for you continually.

Your own, own Sister.

EAS.

8th March

I see you and my darlings in my dreams suffering and sorry—this is about the time you will receive my first letters——

∾∾∾

18th April[95]

Many a long day since your own Sis held the pen—the very day Anna left her bed, I had to go in her place—Oh, my! The patience and more than human kindness of these dear Filicchis for us! You would say it was our Savior Himself they received in his poor and sick strangers. Now I am able to leave my room after my 20 days (as Anna had hers).

This evening standing by the window, the moon shining full on Filicchi's countenance, he raised his eyes to Heaven and showed me how to make the *Sign of the CROSS*. Dearest Rebecca, I was cold with the awful impression that my first making it gave me. The Sign of the CROSS of Christ on me! Deepest thoughts came with it—of I know not what earnest desires to be closely united with Him who died on it—of that last day when He is to bear it in triumph, and did you notice, my dear one, the letter **T** with which the Angel is to mark us on the forehead is a cross? All the Catholic religion is full of those [symbolic] meanings which interest me so. Why Rebecca, they believe all we do and suffer, if we offer it for our sins, the suffering serves to expiate them. You may remember when I asked Mr. Hobart what was meant by *fasting* in our prayer book, as I found myself on Ash Wednesday morning saying so foolishly to God, "I turn to you in

[95] 2.14, *Seton Collected Writings*, 1:296.

fasting, weeping, and mourning." Yet I had come to church with a hearty breakfast of buckwheat cakes and coffee, full of life and spirits, with little thought of my sins.

You may remember what he said about it [fasting] being old customs, etc. Well the dear Mrs. Amabilia Filicchi who I am staying with, never eats this season of Lent until after the clock strikes three [in the afternoon] (then the family assembles). She says she offers her weakness and pain of fasting for her sins, united with our Savior's sufferings. I like that very much, but what I like better, my dearest Rebecca, (only think what a comfort) that they go to Mass here every morning. Ah! How often you and I used to give the sigh, and you would press your arm in mine of a Sunday evening and say no more [worship services] until next Sunday, as we turned from the church door which closed on us, (unless a prayer day was given out in the week). Well, here they go to church at 4 every morning, if they please. You know how we were laughed at for running from one church to the other Sacrament Sundays, that we might receive as often as we could. Here people that love God and live a good regular life, can go (tho' many do not do it) yet they can go every day.

O my! I don't know how anybody can have any trouble in this world who believes all these dear Souls believe. If I don't believe it, it shall not be for want of praying. They must be as happy as the Angels almost. Little Anna is quite well now and so am I—but little [immediate] prospect of [returning] home.

Oh, Joy! Joy! Joy! A Captain Blagge will take us to America! Only think of Mr. Filicchi's goodness as this Captain is a very young man and a stranger, and many things of war or danger might happen on the voyage. Mr. Antonio Filicchi will make it with us—Anna is wild with joy—yet, often she whispers to me, "Ma is there no Catholics in America? Ma won't we go to the Catholic Church when we go home?" Sweet darling! She is now out visiting some of the blessed places with Mrs. Amabilia Filicchi, children,[96] and their governess. Would you believe whenever we go to walk, we go first in some church or convent chapel, as we pass which we always foresee by a large CROSS before it, and say some little prayers before we go further. Men do it as well as women. You know with us [Americans], a man

---

[96] At this time Antonio and Amabilia Filicchi had five children ranging from infancy to eight years of age, including a daughter about the same age as Anna Maria Seton.

would be ashamed to be seen kneeling especially on a week day. O my! I shall be with you again—

Two days more and we set out for HOME! This mild heavenly evening puts me in mind of when often you and I have stood, or rather leaned on each other, looking at the setting sun, sometimes with silent tears and sighs for that HOME, where sorrow cannot come. Alas how may I perhaps find mine! Sorrow plenty—I was speaking of it the other evening to Filicchi and he said in his dry English, "My little sister, God, the Almighty, is laughing at you. He takes care of little birds and makes the lilies grow, and you fear He will not take care of you. I tell you, He will take care of you."

So I hope, dearest Rebecca; you know we used to envy them that were poor because they had nothing to do with the world.

Last hour in Leghorn—

Oh think how this heart trembles! Mrs. Amabilia Filicchi came while the stars were yet bright to say we would go to Mass, and she would there part with her Antonio. Oh the admirable woman! As we entered the church[97] [of Sta. Caterina] the cannon of *The Pyomingo,* which would carry us to America, gave the signal to be on board in 2 hours. MY SAVIOUR—MY God! Antonio and his wife, their separation in God and Communion—poor I, [did] not [receive Communion] but did I not beg Him to give me their Faith and promise Him *all* in return for such a gift. Little Anna and I had only strange tears of joy and grief—we leave but dear ashes.[98]

The last adieu of Mrs. Filicchi as the sun rose full on the balcony [of *The Pyomingo*] where we stood, and the last signal of our ship for our parting. Will I ever forget? Now poor Antonio is tearing away [from home and family], and I hastening to you and my angels.

The 18th of April, at half—past four in the morning, my dear brother came to my room to awaken my soul to all its dearest hopes and anticipations. The heaven was bright with stars, the wind fair, and *The Pyamingo's* signal expected to call us on board. Meanwhile the tolling of the bell called us to Mass, and in a few minutes we were prostrate in the presence of God. Oh, my soul, how solemn was that offering—for a blessing on our voyage—for my dear ones, my sisters, and all so dear to me—and more than all, for the souls of my dear husband and father. Earnestly our desires ascended with

[97] The Church of Sta. Caterina was located near the Filicchi home.
[98] The remains of William Magee Seton.

60

the blessed sacrifice [of the Mass], that they might find acceptance through Him who gave Himself for us. Earnestly we desired to be united with Him, and would gladly encounter all the sorrows before us to be partakers of that Blessed Body and Blood. O my God, spare and pity me.

We returned home with hearts full of many sensations. On my part, sorrow at parting with the friends who had been so kind to me, and the dear little angels [Filicchi children] I tenderly love, struggled with the joy of once more embarking for home. While I gave dear Amabilia a farewell embrace in the balcony, the sun rose bright and glorious, and called out thoughts to that hour when the Sun of Righteousness would rise and reunite us forever.

The signal had been given, the waterman waited for us, and my dear brother [Antonio Filicchi] passed the struggle like a man and a Christian—dear manly soul, it indeed appeared to me in the 'image of God.'

Filippo Filicchi and Guy Carleton waited for us at the Health Office, with letters for America.

[Filippo] Filicchi's last blessing to me was as his whole conduct had been—that of the truest friend. Oh, Filicchi, you shall not witness against me. May God bless you forever, and may you shine as the 'stars in glory,' for what you have done for me.

At eight o'clock, was quietly seated with little Anna and dear Antonio, on the quarter deck. The anchor weighed, sails hoisted, and dear "Yo, Yo!" resounding on all sides, brought to remembrance the 2nd October 1803, with a force as strong as could be borne. Most dear Seton, where are you now? I lose sight of the shore that contains your dear ashes, and your soul is in that region of immensity where I cannot find you. My Father and my God! Yet I must always love to retrospect thy wonderful dispensations—to be sent so many thousand miles on so hopeless an errand—to be constantly supported and accompanied by Thy Consoling Mercy, through scenes of trial, which nature alone must have sunk under—to be brought to the light of Thy Truth, notwithstanding every affection of my heart and power of my will was opposed to it—to be succored and cherished by the tenderest friendship, while separated and far from those whom I loved. My Father and my God, while I live, let me praise—while I have my being let me serve and adore Thee.

19th April, 1804.

The Lord is my refuge. My God is the strength of my confidence. If the Lord had not helped me, it had not failed but my soul had been put to silence; but when I said my foot had slipped, Thy Mercy, O Lord, held me up.[99] For four days past, the trial has been hard. Oh, Lord, deal not with me in displeasure. Let not my enemy triumph—have mercy on us, for Jesus Christ's sake.

So many days on board, and could not find courage to begin my journal.

O my God! Graciously hear my prayers; accept my tears. Shouldst thou deal with us as we deserve, where should we hide from Thy Presence? Lift us from the dust, thou Lord of Righteousness, and though we are tied and bound by the chains of our sins, let the faithfulness of Thy Mercy loose us for the sake of Jesus Christ our Saviour.

20th April—This day thirty-seven years ago, my Seton was born. Does he pass this birthday in heaven? Oh, my husband, how my soul would rejoice to be united with yours—if rejoicing before His Throne, how joyful—if in the bonds of justice, how willingly it would share your pain to lessen it. My Saviour and my God, be not angry with me; consider my desire and have mercy.

My dear, dear little children, no feast of mirth today; my own Rebecca, sister of my soul, something strongly tells me that you, too, are in heaven.

21st—'Ye shall not be tempted above what ye are able, but with the temptation there shall be a way to escape.' This way, Lord, I must seek or I am lost; there is no possibility of outward means, and in Thy Holy Name alone must be my refuge. Once more then, we set out again—(✛ to God is the mark)—trusting in Thee alone, under Thy banner and bearing Thy cross. Since we cannot fly [away from] the monster [Satan], we must face him, calling on Thy Name, Jesus! Jesus! Jesus!

The madness that leads us from Thee is without excuse, the blindness that keeps us from following Thee, leaves us a prey to the destroyer; but, O Lord, let it be so no longer; have mercy upon us and strengthen our souls, or all our resolutions will prove but delusive words. Lord Jesus Christ,

---

[99] Cf. Ps. 46 and Ps. 38:16.

have mercy. When a soul whose only hope is in God, whose concern and desires are so limited that it would forsake all human beings, and account the dearest ties of life as foolishness compared with His Love—when this soul sincerely desirous of serving and obeying Him, is beset by the lowest passions of human nature, and from tears and prayers of earnest penitence can, by the apparently, most trivial incitements, pass to the most humiliating compliances to sin—apparently, for until the effects are experienced, it would be too incredible that the commonest affections and unintentional actions should produce a confusion and disturbance in the mind that is exalted to the love of God, and destroy every impression but momentary gratification—this can only be the work of the enemy of our souls—our souls that have so often declared inviolable fidelity to God—so often prayed to Him for grace and mercy, and while lamenting our errors, and trying to gain mutual strength, have solemnly declared that we would embrace our cross, follow our Leader, and valiantly oppose the enemy of our salvation. Most dear Antonio, a thousand times endeared to me by the struggles of your soul, our Lord is with us—once more the mark is—✝ to God.

23rd—We have passed this day opposite the Pyrenees. Their base, black as jet, and the dazzling whiteness of the snow on their tops, which were high above the clouds that settled round them, formed a subject for the most delightful contemplations, and spoke so loudly of God, that my soul answered them involuntarily in the sweet language of praise and glory. The gentlest motion of the waves, which were as a sheet of glass reflecting the last rays of the sun over the mountains, and the rising moon on the opposite shore—and more than all, that cheerful content in my soul that always accompanies it when it is faithful to its dear Master, has recalled the remembrance of precious hours, and makes me incessantly cry out, "My God! My God! Do not forsake me!" For certain it is, that whatever enjoyments are separate from that heavenly peace His Favor gives, are only bitterness to me, even whilst their delusions would make me forget the only Source of all blessing. The Pyrenees divide Spain and Portugal from France—and Oh! how many miles divide me from the dear Highlands of Home. If the Pyrenees would form a bridge for me, what hardships would I think too great in crossing them. God—Patience—Hope.

24th April—We have passed the straits,[100] and again I have seen Gibraltar, with the thousand bitter recollections that must always recur to

[100] Straits of Gibraltar.

my thoughts when I think of the sufferings of my William when we passed it together.

I have not mentioned two days which I wish to remember—one in view of the towering Alps, which separate Italy from France; also the day we were becalmed opposite the town of Valencia, and surrounded by Lord Nelson's fleet.[101] We were boarded by [military parties from] the *Belle-Isle*, and the evening before by [more of the same from] the seventy-four gun ship *Excellent*.

Oh, my God, if I should die in the midst of so much sin and so little penitence! How terrible it will be to fall into Thy Hands! I have sinned against heaven and before Thee, O my Father. Oh that I could wash out my sins with my tears, and expiate them with my blood. I know I deserve death as the punishment of my sins, and therefore accept with submission the decree of Thy Justice; let this body formed of the earth return to the earth, but oh, let the soul created in Thy Image, return again to Thy Bosom. My hope, O Father of mercies, is in Thee, for I know thou desirest not the death of a sinner, but would rather he should be converted and live. While I receive from Thy Hand the stroke of death, I will bless Thee and hope in Thee. Oh, that I may bless and love Thee eternally, and be accepted through the merits of Jesus Christ. Let me never forget this Mercy above all mercies, and though shame and sorrow must attend the recollection, let it be always present to me that I have been so blinded by sin as to forget its deformity—that upright soul so in love with its God and devoted to His service could forget His Presence and laugh while He was angry—and if He then had left me, how dreadful would have been my fall. Oh, my merciful Saviour, in that hour of darkness Thy Beloved Voice still called and invited me back, and when prostrate on my face in sorrow, and shame, lifted me from the dust, and led me back to Thy fold, so gently, so mercifully, as if my wickedness was to be rewarded instead of punished. Shall I ever be so wretched as to leave Thee again? O my God! My God! Save me from this worst of misery.

25th—Lord of all mercy, I have sinned, I have offended Thee, and the remembrance of my sins and offences overpowers my soul with sorrow; often I have confessed them, and detested them, as I have thought, with

---

[101] Lord Horatio Nelson was a British admiral who won fame as a leading naval commander during the Napoleonic Wars. Both the *HMS Belleisle* and the *HMS Excellent* were 74-gun ships.

real sincerity of heart—still they are ever before me, and what shall I say to Thee, Lord of all mercy? What can I do but throw myself again at Thy feet, and implore Thy pity on a soul whose only hope is in Thy Mercy, and the merits and sufferings of its Redeemer! Vouchsafe to apply them to that poor, afflicted soul, to cleanse it from its iniquities. It is by Thy Blood alone, adored Redeemer, they can be pardoned. Give it a sincere sorrow, and a constant, effectual resolution to avoid all occasions of offending Thee, and seal its pardon through thy infinite merits and righteousness.

I am ashamed, O Lord, to come to Thee, even to thank Thee for Thy Mercy—THY MERCY in so long having patience with my repeated sins and disobedience to Thy Holy Word—but whatever I am, though so miserable and hateful even to my guilty self, thy attributes can never change, Thy Goodness and Mercy know no bounds, and feeling as I do, that I am entirely unworthy even to speak of Thee, yet if even now my poor soul is condemned, if this day is the last of my wretched life on earth, my soul must still praise Thee for so long sparing the punishment so justly due it, must still adore that infinite Mercy that has given me so many means of grace, though my corrupt nature has made so bad a use of them. Oh, Lord Jesus Christ, still be merciful to a miserable sinner.

12th of May, 1804.

The coral in the ocean is a branch of pale green. Take it from its native bed, it becomes firm, bends no more, it is almost a rock. Its tender color is changed to a brilliant red: so too we, submerged in the ocean of this world, subjected to the succession of the waves, ready to give up under the stress of each wave and temptation.

But as soon as our soul rises, and it breathes toward heaven, the pale green of our sickly hopes is changed into that pure bright red of Divine and Constant Love. Then we regard the disruptions of nature and the fall of worlds with a constant and unshakeable confidence.

4th June 1804[102]

Do I hold my dear ones again in my bosom?[103] Has God restored all my Treasure—even the little soul (infant Rebecca) I have so long contemplated as an angel in heaven! Nature cries out they are fatherless, while God himself replies: "I am the Father of the fatherless, and the Helper of the helpless." My God, well may I cling to Thee for "whom have I in Heaven but Thee and who upon Earth beside thee, my heart and my flesh fail, but Thou art the Strength of my heart and my portion forever."[104]

My soul's Sister [her sister-in-law Rebecca] came not out to meet me. She, too, had been journeying fast to her heavenly home and her spirit now seemed only to wait the consoling love and tenderness of her beloved Sister [herself, Elizabeth] to accompany it in its passage to Eternity—to meet her who had been the dear companion of all the pains—and all the comforts— of songs of praise and notes of sorrow, the dear, faithful, tender friend of my Soul, through every varied scene of many years of trial—gone—only the shadow remaining—and that in a few days must pass away.

The home of plenty and of comfort, the Society of Sisters united by prayer and divine affections, the evening hymns, the daily lectures, the sunset contemplations, the Service of Holy Days, the Kiss of Peace, the widows visits—all—all—gone—forever. Is poverty and sorrow the only exchange [for] my Husband—my Sisters—my Home—my comforts? Poverty and sorrow—well with God's blessing, you, too, shall be changed into dearest friends. To the world you show your outward garments, but through them you discover to my soul, the palm of victory, the triumph of Faith, and the sweet footsteps of my Redeemer, leading directly to His Kingdom. Then let me gently meet you, be received in your bosom, and be daily conducted by your counsels through the remainder of the destined journey. I know that many Divine Graces accompany your path, and change the stings of penance, for the ease of conscience and the solitude of the desert, for the Society of Angels. The Angels of God accompanied the faithful when the light of His Truth only dawned in the world—and now, that the Dayspring from on high has visited and exalted our nature to a union with the Divine, will these beneficent beings be less associated or delighted to dwell with the

---

[102] 3.1, *Seton Collected Writings*, 1: 307.

[103] Elizabeth is reunited with her four other children who had remained in New York with relatives.

[104] Ps. 73:25-26.

soul that is panting for heavenly joys, and longing to join in their eternal Alleluias. Oh, no! I will imagine them always surrounding me and in every moment I am free, will sing with them "Holy, Holy, Holy, Lord God of Hosts, heaven and earth is full of Thy Glory."

Sunday morning [July 8]

This is my Rebecca's Birthday in heaven.[105] No more watching now, my darling, Sister. No more agonizing sufferings. The hourly prayers, interrupted by pains and tears, are now exchanged for the eternal Alleluia. The Blessed Angels who have so often witnessed our feeble efforts, now teach your soul the Songs of Sion. Dear, dear Soul, we shall no more watch the setting sun on our knees, and sigh our soul to the Sun of Righteousness, for he has received you to His Everlasting Light. No more sing praises gazing on the moon, for you have awakened to Eternal Day. That dear voice that soothed the widow's heart, admonished the forgetful soul, inspired the love of God, and only uttered sounds of love and peace to all, shall now be heard no more among us, but the reward of those who lead others to Righteousness now crowns His Promise who has said "they shall shine as the stars forever."[106]

The dawning day was unusually clear, and as the clouds received the brightness of the rising sun, Rebecca's soul seemed to be aroused from the slumbers of approaching death, which had gradually composed her during the night, and pointing to a glowing cloud opposite her window, she said with a cheerful smile, "Dear Sister, if this glimpse of Glory is so delightful, what must it be in the presence of our God?"

While the sun arose we said our usual prayers, the *Te Deum*, the Fifty-first Psalm, and part of the Communion Service "with Angels, with Archangels, and all the Company of Heaven we praise Thee."[107] She said "this is the dear day of rest. Suppose, Sister, it should be my blessed Sabbath? Oh, how you disappointed me last evening, when you told me my pulse was stronger! But He is faithful that promises—that I may well say." We then talked a little of our tender and faithful love for each other, and earnestly prayed that this dear affection begun in Christ Jesus on earth, might be perfected through Him in Heaven. Now dear Sister, all is ready,

---

[105] Elizabeth's beloved sister-in-law Rebecca Seton died July 8, 1804.

[106] Dan. 12:3

[107] The *Te Deum* is a traditional prayer of praise attributed to Saint Ambrose. Psalm 51, known as the *Miserere*, is a traditional prayer of repentance.

shut the window and lay my head easy, that I may sleep." (These were her express words.) I said, "My love, I dare not move you without some assistance." "Why not?" she repeated, "All is ready." (She knew that I feared the consequence of moving her.) At this moment Aunt Farquhar[108] entered the room. Rebecca was so desirous of being moved that I raised her head and drew her towards me. Nature gave its last sigh. She was gone in five minutes without a groan.

He who searches the heart and knows the spring of each secret affection, He only knows what I lost at that moment, but her unspeakable gain silences nature's voice and the soul presses forward towards the mark and prize of her high calling in Christ Jesus.

---

[108] Elizabeth Curzon Farquhar, aunt to the dying Rebecca and William Magee Seton.

On Faith—to Amabilia Filicchi

Born in Livorno, Italy, Amabilia Baragazzi married Antonio Filicchi October 2, 1794. The couple had ten children but they had five children under age eight by the time the Setons arrived in Italy in November of 1803. The Filicchi family provided hospitality to Elizabeth and Anna Maria (Annina) after the death of William Magee Seton at Pisa in December. Amabilia was a loving wife, mother, and devoted Catholic woman who befriended and profoundly influenced Elizabeth Seton.

The Filicchi family was instrumental in Elizabeth's conversion to Roman Catholicism. The family's solicitude continued throughout Elizabeth's life and beyond. Amabilia and her husband also extended hospitality to William and Richard Seton when they came to apprentice in the Filicchi firm, 1815-1820. The Filicchi family became lifelong friends, confidants, and benefactors to the Setons and later to the Sisters of Charity of St. Joseph's.

The following journal and letter were written by Elizabeth Seton to Amabilia Filicchi during the nine months of her spiritual search, discernment, and decision regarding her religious conversion March 14, 1805. These are the only records which are now extant of these two kindred souls, both mothers, whose friendship and faith were intertwined.

19th July 1804[1]

Here I am dearest Amabilia, Released from the anxious watchful care of my beloved Rebecca,[2] her most lovely soul departed yesterday morning— and with it—but not to stop on all that, which, at last, is all in order since it is the will of our God. I will tell you what I know you have at heart to know—that the impressions of your example and the different scenes I

---

[1] 3.31, *Seton Collected Writings,* 1:367.
[2] Rebecca Seton, sister-in-law, to Elizabeth Seton.

passed through in Leghorn are far from being effaced from my mind, which indeed could not even in the most painful moments of attendance on my beloved Rebecca, help the strong comparison of a sick and dying bed in your happy country where the poor sufferer is soothed and strengthened at once by every help of religion, where the one you call Father of your soul attends and watches it in the weakness and trials of parting nature, with the same care you and I watch our little infant's body in its first struggles and wants on its entrance into life.

Dearest Rebecca, how many looks of silent distress have we exchanged about the Last Passage, this exchange of time for Eternity? To be sure, her uncommon piety and innocence and sweet confidence in God are my full consolation, but I mean to say that a departing soul has so many trials and temptations that, for my part, I go through a sort of agony never to be described, even while to keep up their hope and courage, I appear to them most cheerful—oh my—forgive these melancholy words [but] they were here before I knew it. Your day and mine will come too—if we are but ready!

The children all asleep. This [is] my time of many thoughts. I had a most affectionate note from Mr. Hobart[3] today asking me how I could ever think of leaving the [Episcopal] church in which I was baptized. But though whatever he says to me has the weight of my partiality for him, as well as the respect it seems to me I could scarcely have for anyone else, yet that question made me smile, for it is like saying that wherever a child is born, and wherever its parents placed it, there it will find the truth. He does not hear the droll invitations made to me every day since I am in my little new home and old friends come to see me. It has already happened that one of the most excellent women I ever knew, who is of the Church of Scotland,[4] finding me unsettled about the great object of a True Faith, said to me, "Oh do, dear Soul, come and hear our Rev. John Mason[5] and I am sure you will join us." A little after, came one I loved for the purest and most innocent manners of the Society of Quakers, (to which I have been always attached), she coaxed me, too, with artless persuasion: "Betsy, I tell thee, thee had best come with us." And my faithful old friend Mrs. T of the Anabaptist

[3] Rev. Henry Hobart was a family friend of the Setons, a curate a Trinity Episcopal Church in New York, and also Elizabeth Seton's spiritual director until 1805.
[4] The Presbyterian Church.
[5] Rev. John Mason was pastor of the Scotch Presbyterian Church in New York. He was known for being an excellent preacher.

meeting says with tears in her eyes, "Oh could you be regenerated! Could you know our experiences and enjoy with us our heavenly banquet." My good mammy, Mary the Methodist, groans and contemplates, as she calls it, over my soul, so misled, because I have yet no convictions.

But oh, my Father and my God, all that will not do for me—Your word is truth, and without contradiction wherever it is, one Faith, one hope, one baptism I look for, wherever it is and I often think my sins, my miseries hide the light, yet I will cling and hold to my God to the last gasp begging for that light and never change until I find it.

August 28th

Long since I wrote you the little word, for there is a sad weariness now over life [which] I never before was tired with. My lovely children around their writing table or around our evening fire, make me forget a little this unworthy dejection, which rises, I believe, from continual application of mind to these multiplied books brought for my [religious] instruction, above all Newton's *Prophecies*.[6] Your poor friend, though, is not so easily troubled as to the facts it dwells on, because it may or may not be, but [having] lived all my days in the thought that all and everybody would be saved who meant well, it grieves my very soul to see that Protestants, as well as your (as I thought hard and severe principles), see the thing so differently. Since this book so valued by them, sends all followers of the Pope to the bottomless pit etc., and it appears, by the account made of them from the Apostles time, that a greater part of the world must be already there, at that rate—

Oh my! The worshipper of images and the Man of Sin are different enough from the beloved souls I knew in Leghorn, to ease my mind in that point, since I so well knew what you worshipped, my Amabilia. Yet so painful and sorrowful an impression is left on my heart, it is all clouded and troubled, so I say the Penitential Psalms if not with the spirit of the royal prophet, at least with his tears, which truly mix with the food and water [on] the couch of your poor friend, yet with such confidence in God that it seems to me He never was so truly my Father and my All at any moment of my life.

---

[6] Thomas Newton first published his *Dissertations on the Prophecies* in 1754-1758. Henry Hobart recommended that Elizabeth read this work.

Anna coaxes me when we are at our evening prayers to say the *Hail Mary* and all say, "Oh do, Ma, teach it to us." Even little Bec[7] tries to lisp it, though she can scarcely speak. I ask my Saviour, why should we not say it, if anyone is in heaven His Mother must be there. Are the Angels then, who are so often represented as being so interested for us on earth, more compassionate or more exalted than she is? Oh no no, Mary our Mother, that cannot be, so I beg her with the confidence and tenderness of her child to pity us, and guide us to the true faith if we are not in it, and if we are, to obtain peace for my poor soul, that I may be a good Mother to my poor darlings. For I know if God should leave me to myself after all my sins, He would be justified. Since I read these books, my head is quite bewildered about the few [souls] that are saved; so I kiss Mary's picture [which] you gave me, and beg her to be a Mother to us.

September–

I have just now the kindest letter from your Antonio. He is still in Boston and would not have been well pleased to see me in Saint Paul's Church[8] today, but peace and persuasion about proprieties etc., over prevailed. Yet I got in a side pew which turned my face towards the Catholic Church[9] in the next street, and found myself twenty times speaking to the Blessed Sacrament there, instead of looking at the naked altar where I was or minding the routine of prayers. Tears plenty, and sighs as silent and deep as when I first entered your blessed Church of Annunciation[10] in Florence, all turning to the one only desire to see the way most pleasing to my God, whichever that way is. Mr. Hobart says, "How can you believe that there are as many gods as there are millions of altars and tens of millions of blessed hosts all over the world?" Again I can but smile at his earnest words, for the whole of my cogitations about it are reduced to one thought—is it GOD who does it, the same God who fed so many thousands with the little barley loaves and little fishes,[11] multiplying them, of course, in the hands which distributed them? The thought stops not a moment to me, I look straight at my GOD and see that nothing is so very hard to believe in it, since it is He who does it.

---

[7] Elizabeth Seton's youngest daughter Rebecca was only two years old.
[8] Saint Paul's Episcopal Chapel on Broadway in New York.
[9] Saint Peter's Catholic Church on Barclay Street.
[10] SS. Annunziata.
[11] Cf. John 5:1-15.

Years ago I read in some old book [that] when you say a thing is a miracle and you do not understand it, you say nothing against the mystery itself, but only acknowledge your limited knowledge and comprehension which does not understand a thousand things you must yet own to be true. So often it comes in my head [that] if the religion which gives to the world, (at least to so great a part of it), the heavenly consolations attached to the belief of the Presence of God in the Blessed Sacrament, to be the food of the poor wanderers in the desert of this world as well as the manna was [for] the support of the Israelites through the wilderness to their Canaan,[12] if this religion says your poor friend is the work and contrivance of men and priests, as they say, then God seems not as earnest for our happiness as these contrivers, nor to love us, though the children of Redemption and bought with the Precious Blood of his dear Son, as much as He did the children of the Old Law since He leaves our churches with nothing but naked walls and our altars unadorned with either the Ark[13] which His Presence filled, or any of the precious pledges of His Care of us which He gave to those of old.

They tell me I must worship Him now in spirit and truth,[14] but my poor spirit very often goes to sleep, or roves about like an idler for want of something to fix its attention. For the truth, dearest Amabilia, I think I feel more true union of heart and soul with Him over a picture of the Crucifixion I found years ago in my Father's portfolio than in the—but what I was going to say would be folly, for truth does not depend on the people around us, or the place we are in. I can only say [that] I do long and desire to worship our God in Truth, and if I had never met you Catholics, and yet should have read the books Mr. Hobart has brought me, they would have in themselves, brought a thousand uncertainties and doubts in my mind. And these soften my heart so much before God in the certainty how much He must pity me, knowing as He does the sole and whole bent of my Soul is to please Him only, and get close to Him in this life and the next. In the midnight hour, believe me, I often look up at the walls through the tears and distress that overpowers me, expecting rather to see His finger writing on the wall[15] for my belief than that He will forsake or abandon so poor a creature.

---

[12] Cf. Exodus 16.
[13] Cf. Exodus 25:8; 40:34.
[14] John 4:23.
[15] Cf. Daniel 5:5.

November 1ˢᵗ—All Saints

I do not get on Amabilia—cannot cast the balance for the peace of this Poor Soul, but it suffers plenty, and the body, too. I say daily with great confidence of being one day heard, the 119ᵗʰ Psalm,[16] [and now am] never weary of repeating it and reading Kempis,[17] who by the way was a Catholic writer, and in our Protestant preface says "wonderfully versed in the knowledge of the Holy Scriptures." I read much, too, of Saint Francis de Sales[18] [who was] so earnest for bringing all to the bosom of the Catholic Church. I say to myself, will I ever know better how to please God than they did? And down I kneel to pour my tears to them and beg them to obtain faith for me—then I see FAITH is a gift of God to be diligently sought and earnestly desired, and groan to Him for it in silence, since our Saviour says I cannot come to Him unless the Father draws me. So it is—by and by, I trust this storm will cease, how painful and often agonizing. He only knows, who can and will; still it in His own good time.

Mrs. Eliza Sadler, my long tried friend, observed to me this morning [that] I had penance enough without seeking it among Catholics. True but we bear all the pain without the merit. Yet I do try sincerely to turn all mine for account of my soul. I was telling her [that] I hoped the more I suffered in this life, the more I hoped to be spared in the next, as I believed God would accept my pains in atonement for my sins. She said indeed that was a very comfortable doctrine. She wished she could believe it. Indeed it is all my comfort, dearest Amabilia. Worn out now to a skeleton almost, death may over take me in my struggle, but God himself must finish it.

January 1805

Many a long day since I wrote you, dear friend, for this perpetual routine of life with my sweet darlings says the same thing every day for the exterior, except that our old servant has had a long sickness and I have had the comfort to nurse her night and day as well as do her work of all kinds for the snow has been almost impassably high and even my precious sister, Mary Post, could not get to see us. You would not say we were not happy, for the love with which it is all seasoned can only be enjoyed by those who could experience our reverse, but we never give it a sigh. I play the piano

---

[16] Psalm 120 in contemporary Catholic Bibles.

[17] Author of the *Imitation of Christ*.

[18] Author of many works including *Introduction to the Devout Life* (1609) and *Treatise on the Love of God* (1616).

all the evening for them and they dance, or we get close round the fire and I live over with them all the scenes of David, Daniel or Judith,[19] etc. until we forget the present entirely. The neighbors' children, too, beset us to hear our stories, sing our hymns, and say prayers with us—dear dearest Amabilia, God will at last deliver.

Now I read with an agonizing heart the Epiphany Sermon of Bourdaloue. "Alas, where is my star?"[20] I have tried so many ways to see the Dr. O'Brien whom they say is the only Catholic priest in New York, where they say Catholics are the offscourings[21] of the people. Somebody said their congregation is "a public nuisance" but that troubles me not. The congregation of a city, may be very shabby yet very pleasing to God, or very bad people among them, yet cannot hurt the faith as I take it. Should the priest himself deserve no more respect than is here allowed him, his ministry of the sacraments would be the same to me if, dearest friend, I ever shall receive them. I seek but God and his church and expect to find my peace in them, not in the people.

Would you believe, Amabilia, in a desperation of heart I went last Sunday to Saint George's [Episcopal] Church.[22] The wants and necessities of my soul were so pressing that I looked straight up to God, and I told him, "Since I cannot see the way to please You, Whom Alone I wish to please, everything is indifferent to me. Until You do show me the way You mean me to walk in, I will trudge on in the path You suffered me to be born in, and go even to the very sacrament where I once used to find You." So away I went. My old mammy, [was] happy to take care of the children for me once more, till I came back. But if I left the house a Protestant, I returned to it a Catholic, I think—since I determined to go no more to the Protestants, being much more troubled than ever I thought I could be, while I remembered GOD IS MY GOD—but so it was that the bowing of my heart before the Bishop[23] to receive his Absolution which is given publicly and universally to all in the church [at Episcopalian worship service], I had

---

[19] From the Sacred Scriptures.

[20] The scriptural allusion to the Epiphany star refers to Matthew. 2:2, Elizabeth was reading one of the sermons of Louis Bourdaloue, a 17th century French spiritual writer, whose collected sermons delivered in Paris fill dozens of volumes.

[21] Outcasts or marginalized of society.

[22] Saint George's was a daughter chapel of Trinity Parish, and was located at Second Avenue and 14th Street near Stuyvesant Square.

[23] Bishop Benjamin Moore of the Episcopal Church.

not the least faith in his prayer, and looked for an apostolic loosing from my sins, which by the books, Mr. Hobart had given me to read, I find they do not claim or admit.

Then trembling to Communion half-dead with the inward struggle, when they said the "Body and Blood of Christ"—Oh Amabilia, no words for my trial! And I remember in my old Prayerbook, of former edition when I was a child, it was not as now, said to be spiritually taken and received—however to get thoughts away, I took the Daily Exercise of good Abbé Plunkett[24] to read the prayers after COMMUNION, but finding every word addressed to Our Dear Saviour as really present and conversing with it, I became half-crazy, and for the first time, could not bear the sweet caresses of the darlings or bless their little dinner. O my God, that day! But it finished calmly at last abandoning all to God, and a renewed confidence in the Blessed Virgin whose mild and peaceful love reproached my bold excesses, and reminded me to fix my heart above with better hopes.

Now they tell me [to] take care [because] I am a Mother, and I must answer for my children in Judgment, whatever Faith I lead them to. That being so, and I so unconscious, for I little thought until told by Mr. Hobart that their Faith could be so full of consequence to them or me, I WILL GO PEACEABLY and FIRMLY TO THE CATHOLIC CHURCH—for if Faith is so important to our salvation, I will seek it where true Faith first began and seek it among those who received it from GOD HIMSELF. The controversies on it I am quite incapable of deciding, and as the strictest Protestant allows Salvation to a good Catholic, to the Catholics I will go, and try to be a good one. May God accept my intention and pity me. As to supposing the word of our Lord has failed, and that He suffered his first foundation to be built on by Antichrist, I cannot stop on that without stopping on every other Word of Our Lord and being tempted to be no Christian at all. For if the First Church became Antichrist, and the second holds her rights from it, then I should be afraid both might be Antichrist, and I make my way to the bottomless pit by following either.

Come then, my little one, we will go to Judgment together, and present Our Lord his own words. If he says, "You fools, I did not mean that," we will say: "Since You said You would be always even to the end of ages with this church [which] You built with Your Blood, if You ever left it,

---

[24] Rev. Peter Plunkett was an Irish priest and apologist whom Elizabeth met in Leghorn.

it is Your Word which misled us. Therefore, please to pardon Your poor fools for Your own Words sake."

I am between laughing and crying all the while, Amabilia, yet not frightened. For on God Himself I pin my Faith—and wait only the coming of your Antonio, whom I look for next week from Boston, to go valiantly and boldly to the standard of the Catholic, and trust all to God. It is His Affair NOW.

[February 27th 1805, Ash Wednesday]

A day of days for me, Amabilia, I have been—where?—to the Church of Saint Peter[25] with a CROSS on the top instead of a weathercock[26]—that is mischievous, but I mean [that] I have been to what is called here among so many churches, the Catholic church. When I turned the corner of the street it is in, "Here, my God, I go," said I, "heart all to you." Entering it, how that heart died away as it were in silence before the little tabernacle and the great Crucifixion [painting] over it.[27] "Ah, My God, here let me rest," said I, and down [went] the head on the bosom and the knees on the bench. If I could have thought of anything but God, there was enough I suppose to have astonished a stranger, by the hurrying over one another of this offscoured congregation, but as I came only to visit His Majesty, I knew not what it meant until afterwards. It was a day they receive Ashes [at] the beginning of Lent. The drole but, most venerable Irish priest,[28] who seems [to have] just come there, talked of death so familiarly that he delighted and revived me.

[March 14th 1805]

After all [the worshippers] were gone, I was called to the little room next to the altar and there PROFESSED to believe what the Council of Trent[29] believes and teaches, laughing with my heart to my Saviour, who saw that I knew not what the Council of Trent believed, only that it believed what the Church of God declared to be its belief, and consequently is now my belief. For as to going a walking any more about what all the different

---

[25] Saint Peter's Catholic Church on Barclay Street in lower Manhattan.

[26] Saint Paul's Church where Elizabeth sometimes worshipped had a weathercock at the top of its steeple instead of a cross. This is the same church which was used as a Respite Center for Emergency Teams after the 9/11 attack in 2001.

[27] This painting, which hangs above the Altar of Sacrifice, was executed by the Mexican artist José Vallejo and was a gift from the archbishop of Mexico City in 1789.

[28] Rev. John Byrne.

[29] The Council of Trent was a sixteenth-century ecumenical council of the Catholic Church.

people believe, I cannot, being quite tired out. I came up light at heart and cool of head, the first time these many long months, but not without begging our Lord to wrap my heart deep in that Opened Side so well described in the beautiful Crucifixion, or lock it up in His little tabernacle, where I shall now rest forever. Oh Amabilia, the endearments of this day with the children [when I returned] and the play of the heart with God while keeping up their little farces with them. Anna suspects. I anticipate her delight when I take her [with me] next Sunday.

So delighted now to prepare for this GOOD CONFESSION[30] which, bad as I am, I would be ready to make on the house top to insure the GOOD ABSOLUTION I hope for after it. And then to set out [upon] a new life—a new existence itself. No great difficulty for me to be ready for it, for truly my life has been well called over in bitterness of soul these months of sorrow past.

[March 20th 1805]

IT IS DONE—easy enough—the kindest most respectable confessor is this Mr. O'Brien with the compassion and yet firmness in this work of Mercy which I would have expected from Our Lord Himself. Our Lord Himself I saw alone in him, both in his and my part of this Venerable Sacrament. For, Oh Amabilia, how awful those words of unloosing after a 30 years bondage! I felt as if my chains fell, as those of Saint Peter at the touch of the divine messenger.[31]

My God what new scenes for my Soul—ANNUNCIATION DAY! I shall be made one with Him who said, "Unless you eat My Flesh and drink My Blood you can have no part with ME."[32]

I count the days and hours—yet, a few more of hope and expectation and then. How bright the sun these morning walks of preparation—deep snow, or smooth ice, all to me the same. I see nothing but the little bright cross on Saint Peter's steeple. The children are wild with their pleasure of going with me in their turn.

---

[30] The Sacrament of Reconciliation.

[31] Cf. Acts 7.

[32] Roman Catholics believed that the body and blood of Jesus Christ is present in the Holy Eucharist and received by the faithful in Holy Communion under the form of bread and wine.

25th March

At last, Amabilia—at last—GOD IS MINE and I AM HIS! Now let all go its round—I HAVE RECIEVED HIM! The awful impressions of the evening before, fears of not having done all to prepare, and yet even then, transports of confidence and hope in his GOODNESS—

MY God, to the last breath of life will I not remember this night of watching for morning dawn? The fearful beating heart so pressing to be gone—the long walk to town, but every step counted nearer that street—then nearer that tabernacle, then nearer the moment He would enter the poor, poor, little dwelling so all His Own.

And when He did, the first thought, I remember, was "Let God arise, let his enemies be scattered,"[33] for it seemed to me [that] my King had come to take His throne. Instead of the humble, tender welcome I had expected to give Him, it was but a triumph of joy and gladness that the Deliverer was come, and my defense and shield and strength and Salvation made mine for this world and the next.

Now then all the excesses of my heart found their play, and it danced with more fervor—no, must not say that, but perhaps almost with as much as the royal Prophets before his Ark,[34] for I was far richer than he and more honoured than he ever could be—now the point is for the fruits—so far, truly I feel all the powers of my soul held fast by Him who came with so much Majesty to take possession of this little poor kingdom.

[April 14]

An Easter COMMUNION now—in my green pastures amidst the refreshing waters for which I thirsted truly[35]—but you would not believe how the Holy Week puzzled me, unless at the time of the Divine Sacrifice so commanding, and yet already so familiar for all my wants and necessities. That speaks for itself, and I am all at home in it, but the other hours of the office having no book to explain or lead, I was quite at a loss, but made it up with that only thought, "My God is here, He sees me—every sigh and desire is before Him," and so I would close my eyes and say the dear Litany of JESUS, or some of the Psalms, and most that lovely hymn to the Blessed Sacrament, "FAITH for all defects supplies, and SENSE is lost

---

[33] Possibly a reference to Psalm 82.
[34] Cf. 1 Chronicles 13:8.
[35] Cf. Psalm 23:2.

in MYSTERY—here the Faithful rest secure, while God can Vouch and Faith insure."[36] You would sometimes enjoy through mischief, if you could just know the foolish things that pass my brain after so much Wonderful Knowledge—as I have been taking in it [my mind] about idol worshipping etc., etc., even in the sacred moments of the Elevation, my heart will say half-serious, dare I worship You—Adored Saviour—but He has proved well enough to me there, what He is. I can say with even more transports than Saint Thomas, "MY LORD and MY God"[37]—truly it is a greater Mystery how souls for whom he had done such incomprehensible things, should shut themselves out by incredulity from His best of all Gifts, this Divine Sacrifice and Holy Eucharist, refusing to believe in the spiritual and heavenly order of things, that WORD which spoke and created the Whole Natural Order, recreating through succession of ages for the body. Yet He cannot be believed to recreate for the soul—I see more mystery in this blindness of redeemed souls than in any of the mysteries proposed in his Church—with what grateful and unspeakable joy and reverence I adore the daily renewed virtue of THAT WORD by which we possess Him in our blessed MASS, and Communion—but all that is but words since Faith is from God, and I must but humble myself and adore.

Your Antonio—goes [away] now for England and will soon be with you, I trust. Much he says of my bringing all the children to your Gubbio[38] to find peace and abundance, but I have a long life of sins to expiate. Since I hope always to find the morning MASS in America, it matters little what can happen through the few successive days I may have to live, for my health is pitiful. Yet we will see, perhaps our Lord will pity my little ones. At all events, happen now what will, I rest with GOD—the tabernacle and Communion—so now I can pass [into] the Valley of Death[39] itself.

Antonio will tell you all our little affairs. Pray for your own.

EAS.

---

[36] A traditional Catholic hymn for Benediction of the Blessed Sacrament, *Tantum Ergo*.
[37] Cf. John 20:28.
[38] The Filicchi family was originally from Gubbio in Tuscany and still had relatives there.
[39] Cf. Psalm 23:4.

My very dear Friend,

You must have long ago expected a reply to your last letter of _____, but this is the first opportunity your Antonio has pointed out, and he says the only direct one there has been for some months. Indeed, dear Amabilia, your upright and happy soul can never imagine the struggles and distresses of mine since I left you, or you would not wonder if I avoided writing or speaking on the source of its unhappiness, and certainly it was not easy to write to one as dear to me as you are without expressing it.

All now is past. The heavy cloud has given place to the sunshine of peace. My soul is as free and contented as it has been burdened and afflicted, for God has been so gracious to me as to remove every obstacle in my mind to the True Faith and given me strength to meet the difficulties and temptations I am externally tried with. You may suppose my happiness in being once more permitted to kneel at his altar, and to enjoy those foretastes of Heaven He has provided for us on Earth. Now everything is easy. Poverty, suffering, the displeasure of my friends all lead me to Him, and only fit my heart more eagerly to approach its only Good. How your dear charitable heart so often lifted to God in prayer for me will rejoice. I know that it will with those also of Gubbio[41] who have so tenderly kept a poor stranger in remembrance. If I could make them understand me,[42] I would thank them most affectionately and beg them still to brighten their crown and pray that the one their prayers have helped to gain [the True Faith] for me may not be lost.

Your Antonio[43] is now in Philadelphia. Oh how you would be pleased to see him so well, so handsome, so delighted with your sweet picture as scarcely to permit any one to hold it in their hands. And certainly the expression of it is just such as you would have wished, tender and sorrowful as if lamenting your separation. He feels it so, and speaks as tenderly to it as if you were present. He also talks of his Patrick[44] as if he had seen him but yesterday—of his dancing and shaking himself do drolly and all his little

---

[40] 3.24, *Seton Collected Writings*, 1:353.
[41] Relatives of the Filicchi family.
[42] Elizabeth refers to being understood in English since she was not fluent in Italian.
[43] The husband of Amabilia Filicchi.
[44] Elizabeth Seton had known the two sons of Antonio and Amabilia Filicchi, Patrizio, and Georgio, when she was in Italy.

lovely ways. For me, I always see my Georgino with his dear arms stretched out to me, and sweet inviting smiles. Oh, if ever I should hold him to my heart again, how happy I should be, but that happiness with every other wish and desire must all be referred to Paradise, for here [on earth] in all human probability they will not be accomplished.

Yet, I must often think of you all, of the dear girls and of you, dear Amabilia, and all the unmerited kindness I have received from you. God only can reward you.

Well we may bless Him for keeping your Antonio free from the danger of the [Yellow] Fever in both countries. His health here is so perfect that notwithstanding the severity of the winter, he has not had even a headache, as no doubt he has told you, for he speaks of it as a most gracious Providence. Oh with what a thankful soul I shall adore that Providence if he [Antonio] is only restored safe and well to you. He will tell you that he took the figs and one basket of the raisins you so kindly sent to me, as he wished them for a friend. One basket was abundance for my darlings. I boil them in rice for them and it makes an excellent dinner. You speak with so much ceremony about sending them, my dear friend, that surely I ought to have made many apologies for so great a liberty as I took with you when I sent you some things so trifling. Let not such language be known between us—God sees my heart to you and knows it loves you most sincerely, and respects your virtues more than ever I can express. If ever it is in my power most gladly will I prove it to you.

How much I thank your brother Gaspero[45] for his kind recollections, and beg you will return them for me as also to the dear Rosina and all your family. Antonio knows how often I have wished to transport some fine apples to Dr. Tutilli. His kindness I must always remember with the most lively gratitude and beg you to offer him my affectionate compliments.

Is Sibald and Belfour still of your party? Will you remember me to them? Kiss your darlings for me a thousand times. Little Anna is much improved. She always speaks with delight of Leghorn, and of your dear girls as if she was with them only yesterday. When Antonio showed her your picture, she was in a rapture and said afterwards, "Oh Mamma, how I wish to hold it in my hands and kiss it."

---

[45] Gaspero Baragazzi, Amabilia Filicchi's brother.

Dear, dear Amabilia, may Almighty God bless you. Do remember me particularly to Mr. Hall.[46]

Your

E A Seton

ৡৡৡৡৡৡৡৡৡৡৡ

ৡৡৡৡৡৡ

ৡৡ

---

[46] Rev. Thomas Hall was the British chaplain who attended William Magee Seton on his deathbed in Pisa and conducted his funeral services. Hall lived on the first floor of the same address as Antonio and Amabilia Filicchi, who occupied the second floor. The Setons lived on the third floor during their stay in Leghorn.

On Friendship—to Julianna Scott

Julianna Sitgreaves Scott (1765-1842) was the first daughter of William and Susanna Deshon Sitgreaves. Affectionately known as "Julia," she was born in Philadelphia, Pennsylvania and married a successful and prominent lawyer, Lewis Allaire Scott (1759-1798), January 15, 1785. Lewis Allaire became the secretary of state of New York (1784-1798). The couple had two children, John (Jack) Morin Scott (1789-1858) and Maria Litchfield Scott (178?-1814).

Elizabeth knew Julia as a family friend and mentor. Julia was older than Elizabeth by about ten years. Julia returned to live in Philadelphia after being widowed in March of 1798. Julia remained a lifelong confidante and benefactor of the Setons. Julia was a godparent to Catherine, Elizabeth's second daughter, but was especially fond of Elizabeth's first-born, Anna Maria (Annina) Seton for whose dancing lessons, etc, she sent money.

The following twenty-six letters during the period from 1803 through 1809 are but a sample of over 130 letters exchanged for at least nineteen years between these dear friends. The women shared their hearts with one another.

1st October 1803[1]

1st October 1803[1]

My ever dear Julia,

When I tell you that I have in the month of August weaned a sick baby,[2] broken up housekeeping, and have been ever since in hourly expectation of embarking for Leghorn,[3] you will easily conceive that there has been no possibility of dwelling on the subject in a letter to you. My

---

[1] 1.174, *Seton Collected Writings,* 1:222.

[2] Rebecca Mary Seton, the fifth and last child born to Elizabeth and William Magee Seton.

[3] The Setons sailed to Leghorn on *The Shepherdess* in the hope that the sea voyage would restore William Magee's health.

Seton's decline [of health] is so rapid that there can be no hope of his recovery in the view of MORTAL HOPES, but knowing Who holds the scale, and how merciful is His Guidance, my soul reposes on that Mercy and now feels the full force of those consolations, [which] I have so often wished you to know the value of.

The signal for coming on board [*The Shepherdess*] is already given. All my earthly concerns are settled as if by the hour of death. In this sacred hour my soul implores for you, the friend of my first and warmest affections, that Peace which God alone can give.

Your **EAS.**

William has put up for you a box because it is marked W.E.S.—and a picture he thought you would like. Bless your dear children for me—and my dear Charlotte and Brother Samuel.[4]

28th October 1803[5]

We are now past the western islands[6] which are exactly half way between New York and Leghorn, and hourly expect to meet some vessel that may take our letters home. As I am sure, my very dear Friend, will be among the first inquirers of news from us, I write, although sure there can be little to interest you after saying that my Seton is daily getting better, and that little Anna and myself are well. If I dared indulge my enthusiasm and describe, as far as I could give them words, my extravagant enjoyments in gazing on the [Atlantic] Ocean, and the rising and setting sun, and the moonlight Evenings, a quire[7] of paper would not contain what I should tell you. One subject you will share with me, which engages my whole soul—the dear, the tender, the gracious love with which every moment has been marked in these, my heavy hours of trial.

You will believe because you know how blessed they are who rest on our Heavenly Father—not one struggle, nor desponding thought to contend with—confiding Hope and consoling Peace have attended My

---

[4] Charlotte Sitgreaves Cox and Samuel Sitgreaves, siblings of Julia Sitgreaves Scott.

[5] 2.3, *Seton Collected Writings*, 1:245.

[6] Probably the Azores.

[7] A quire is a collection of approximately 24 sheets of paper of the same size and quality, or one twentieth of a ream.

William through storms and dangers that must have terrified a soul whose Rock is not Christ.

ৡৢৡৢৡৢৡৢ

15th July 1804[8]

My dearest Julia

The tenderness and affection of your expressions brought many quick and bitter tears from my very heart. I find so many changes and reverses in my singular fate that I did not look for your kindness or value your friendship as I ought. Accustomed to find every one occupied in their own concerns, I thought Julia is enjoying and pursuing [hers], and I will not remind her there is a being so burdened with sorrow as I am. My Seton has left his five darlings and myself wholly dependent on the bounty of those individuals who have loved and respected him. Happily for us both, entirely unconscious of the desperate state of his affairs, he died quite happy in the idea that we would have a sufficiency when his books[9] were brought up. On the contrary, there is even a great deficiency, and if John Wilkes did not continue a faithful friend to us, I should see my dear ones in a state of absolute poverty. My brother-in-law [Wright] Post and Mrs. [Sarah] Startin unite with him in our maintenance for this year, as my Rebecca is so young [not yet 3]. After which, if I live, I am to pursue some personal exertion towards it myself.

I am so happy amongst all my difficulties to meet with a small neat house about a half-mile from town, where we occupy the upper room and will let [rent] the lower floor as soon as I can find a tenant. We eat milk, morning and evening, and chocolate for dinner, always with a thankful heart and a good appetite. My dearest companion and friend, my soul's Sister[10] departed for the happier world this day [a] week. With her is gone all my interest in the connections of this life. It appears to me Julia that a cave or a desert would best satisfy my natural desire but God has given me a great deal to do, and I have always, and hope always, to prefer His Will to every wish of my own. He has been most gracious to me in returning [to] me all my dear ones in health, and providing a roof to cover us—most gracious in giving, both to my husband and sister-in-law, that Peace in their last

---

[8] 3.5, *Seton Collected Writings,* 1:313. Elizabeth became a widow the previous December.

[9] Financial records and accounts of Seton, Maitland and Company which was in bankruptcy.

[10] Elizabeth referred to her sister-in-law Rebecca Seton, as her soul's sister.

hours which assures me they are free from all sufferings and inheriting His Promises—most gracious in raising my Soul above all the changing events of my mortal existence. Why then, you will say, my friend, do you declare you are burdened with sorrow? Next week I will write you why.

I anticipate your first question to me, my dear Julia, can you not share with me your portion?[11] Can you not add to the contributions of those friends who support me? In answer to these questions, which I am sure of from you, I assure you, that for the present, there is no necessity. I spend much less than even those friends imagine, and delight in the opportunity of bringing up my children without those pretentions and indulgencies that ruin so many.

Your idea of my making you a visit, you will readily see is impracticable. How much I wish to see your dear children and yourself, I cannot express, but I put that among the many other wishes that I set aside as not to be gratified, for your coming to me at this Season cannot be right. The Father of Blessings bless you, my love, remember me to Charlotte—Hitty and Maria[12] and be assured of my sincere and grateful affection.

28th November 1804[13]

My dear Julia,

You have had time to arrive at home, to be married,[14] according to the report of the world, and to have fulfilled all the etceteras, etceteras, and yet I do not hear from you. Is it true that you are so seriously engaged? Or have you been reading my memorandums and concluded that any intercourse[15] with the mad enthusiast is loss of time? I have been constantly busy with my darlings mending up and turning winter clothes. They have in turn all been sick from the change of weather, added to their whooping cough. The old Mammy, too, has been sick. In short, dear, I have been one

---

[11] Julia invited Elizabeth to come to Philadelphia to live, and in July when she visited New York, Julia tried to persuade Elizabeth to let Anna Maria return with her to Philadelphia.

[12] Julia Scott's sister and niece, Charlotte Sitgreaves Cox and Mehitabel "Hitty" Cox, and her daughter, Maria Litchfield Scott.

[13] 3.13, *Seton Collected Writings,* 1:334.

[14] She visited Elizabeth in September but Julia never remarried.

[15] Intercourse was the term commonly used during the nineteenth century for social or business interactions between persons or groups.

of Job's Sisters—and from all appearances must long look to his example.[16] Well, I am satisfied "to sow in tears if I may reap in joy," and when all the wintry storms of time are past we shall enjoy the delights of an Eternal Spring.[17] In the meantime, I should wish to know if you are alive, how your domestic affairs (in which you interested me very much) go on. Something about you all, but more than all, a little of your dear interior self would be most acceptable as your soul is most dear to me, dear Julia. In that only can I hope to perpetuate my affection for you, as in all exteriors, we are and must, continue to be wholly separated.[18] There is nothing new in my prospects since your departure except a suggestion of Mr. [John] Wilkes that in order to avoid the boarding school plan I might receive boarders from one curate of Saint Marks[19] who has ten or twelve scholars, and lives in the vicinity of the city—which would produce at least a part of the necessary means to make the ends of this year meet with my manner of living. Antonio Filicchi has not returned from Boston. His letters are full of extravagancies, very much the reverse of the above ideas, such as my heart would grasp at, but reason must not listen to. God Almighty will, I trust, direct it. My mind is but little occupied with the subject, so much I confide in His pitying Mercy——

Your and Maria's visits to me last summer appears like a vision. Little Kit often speaks of Aunt Scott and Anna sighs so pitifully at the mention of your name, that my heart involuntarily answers hers, and though fully convinced in every point of view of the value of your affectionate kindness to her, nature will sometimes prove her power and I shrink from the promise which reason and gratitude has sealed. She is a singular child and requires so many amendments in her disposition and habits, that I fear she will call the whole force of your affection for me in exercise, but do not think of it. God will bless your kind intentions to a fatherless child—and however rough or unhinged my mind may be, my Soul must be attached to you tenfold forever.

---

[16] Cf. Job 1.

[17] Psalm 126:5.

[18] Elizabeth Seton encouraged Julia Scott to be attuned to matters of the heart and her relationship with God.

[19] Rev. William Harris conducted a school associated with Saint Mark's Episcopal Church, a daughter church of Trinity Parish.

Remember me to your children and Mother[20]—and affectionately to Charlotte [Cox] and Brother Sam [Sitgreaves].

Your *EAS*

৵৻৵৻৵৻

13th December 1804[21]

Your letter, my dearest Julia, should have been answered immediately, and would have been, if I could have commanded the time for writing as readily as my heart dictated, but in this as in many other instances, it must trust to your goodness whilst it is fully sensible how little it deserves the tenderness of your friendship. Your gift of love[22] to my dear ones will, I fear, be expended in wood and bread for us all. For with even [penny-]pinching economy, those two articles must be very heavy. All goes infinitely better than I could have expected. While my health is so much mended, that blessing supplies the place of many. Yet dear, if you could see your friend turn out at day light in the coldest mornings, make fire, dress and comb, wash and scold the little ones, fill the kettle, prepare breakfast, sweep, make beds, and the etcetera work, nurse the old woman, keep the school [at home], make ready dinner, supper and put to bed again, you will say, could she go through it, all the while looking up, too. This I am always liable to, as my poor old woman, is subject to complaints which have confined her in bed for a week together during the severest weather. You will say, where are all the friends, but must consider everyone has their own occupations and pursuits and often for ten and twelve day[s], I see no one. My Italian friend [Antonio Filicchi] has been detained in Boston, but doubtless will soon be on his way to your city and, of course, introduced to you.

Your visionary scheme of love and kindness, like many other sweet imaginations, will do to dream of. While I am in this part of the world, where my sister is, there I must be. Julia, Julia, dear Julia, do not forget my question, and when you imagine the voice, let it be animated by love, entreaty, supplication for, oh, when I think of you in that point of view, I could fasten you in my bosom and drag you, compel you, and when sure of your consent, fly with you to the feet of Our Saviour and Judge. Yes, Judge, He must and will be, and then, though I should be eager to share

[20] Susanna Deshon Sitgreaves.
[21] 3.14, *Seton Collected Writings*, 1:336.
[22] Julia regularly sent Elizabeth financial contributions for the family.

my oil with you, I shall find there is only enough for my own little lamp.[23] Dear, dear, dear friend consider, and when you consider, resolve, and then quickly go to Him. Tell Him you are in want of everything. Beg for the new heart, the right spirit, and that He will teach you to do the thing that pleases Him.[24]

Well, there are fine Preachers in this life, but my dearest, if you possessed a little glass through which you could discern the finest country, and one you tenderly loved neglected to look through it, and would perhaps forget the way, you would be ready even to pain them rather than let them wait till the clouds and storms gathered round and the road should be either hidden or lost. If you take your darlings astray, too, take care, Miss Julia! You say write—I will indeed when I can, even though it should be a scrawl like this as fast as the pen can drive. There is nothing more done in the new arrangement, but I believe it will certainly take place. How I wish John Wilkes and yourself had been cut out for each other—but perhaps you have already chained the bachelor. You said you were not afraid in the main point. Write to me, tell me—send my papers, and be assured of the tenderest affection of your

EAS.

ๆๆๆๆๆๆ

March 5th 1805[25]

My dearest Julia,

It is almost incredible that your most affectionate letter has been six weeks in my possession unanswered. The love and tenderness it expresses brought me to my knees. I ask God with tears of joy and thankfulness have I indeed such a friend? Indeed, Julia, it has made me saucy, for my mind often involuntarily turns to some pleasures, which before I should not have had a thought of accomplishing—not exactly those you wished for me, for it seems I must fulfill the engagement with Mr. [John] Wilkes. But I think in consequence of your generosity and love, I may procure a person who will rid me of the dreaded burden of patching and darning, and that I may be able to give a large portion of my time to my Anna in communicating

---

[23] See Matthew 25: 1-13.
[24] See Ezekiel 36:26.
[25] 3.19, *Seton Collected Writings,* 1:344.

to her what I know of Music and French, which is as much and perhaps more than she would attain in another situation. I am persuaded, and have experienced, that in those acquirements which require so much patience and application, a Mother is by far the most desirable preceptress. At least I have an earnest wish to make the experiment with her and think I can trust to my sense of duty to her and to you, who will afford me the means for a regular attention on my part. Therefore, dearest friend, let your three hundred be 150 dollars, which will amply pay the woman and supply Anna with clothing.

I have run the gauntlet, and persuaded Antonio Filicchi that this is not the time for my entering into his fascinating schemes, tho' I do not see my duty to my dear ones in a clear view either way. I could go almost mad at the view of the conduct of every friend I have here except yourself. It would really seem that in their estimation, I am a child not to be trusted with its daily bread, least it should waste it—but never mind, all will come right one of these days. You know penance is the purifier of the soul, therefore I drive every thought away, and meet it all with the smile of content, which however often conceals the sharp thorn in the heart. A thorn I can give you no name for. I should be sorry to think it pride or disappointment, for I can have no claim on anyone except what God opens their hearts to do for me. Peace, peace, rebellious Nature—how much worse do you deserve.

Your assurance of dear Brother's [Samuel] interest in me and my affairs brought home many a remembrance of time past. I can see him, speak to him, read his heart, and would throw myself upon his pity and affection securely and without reserve as if I was still his little Betty Bayley. But that too must be hushed, and I must jog on the allotted path through all its windings and weariness till it brings me home where all tears shall be wiped away, and sorrow and sighing be heard no more.[26] In the meanwhile, dearest, courage, LOOK UP.

Is your dear little heart still filled with contradictions? Or has the birth of the new darling been propitious?[27] How I should like to witness your every day scene without your knowing it. Dearest Julia, I fear it would present a picture less free from care than even my own, yet your Maria must be a precious blessing to you, [and] I hope [she] will be the friend of your heart and your comfort. My Anna is almost an angel to me.

---

[26] Cf. Revelation 21:4.

[27] Possibly the child of Julia's niece, Hitty Cox Markow, who was married the previous year.

Antonio Filicchi will present this to you. You will find him very much the gentleman, but too diffident a character to engage acceptance on first acquaintance, tho I am sure you will give him credit for the excellent qualities I have found in him. For my sake, show him your affable side, as his curiosity is really excited with respect to you.

Dear, dear, dear, Julia, what will you think of my not writing you? Tho indeed if you knew the daily domestic scene you would soon forgive. The old Mammy is half her time sick, her Daughter lain-in' in my house with many other Etceteras[28]—yet do not think this a picture of my soul. It is as quiet as your tenderest affection could wish it. With its tenderest affections prays for the peace of yours, and that the same Sheltering Wing may at length receive us both—united forever.

Your *EAS.*

March 25th

6th May 1805[29]

Dear dearest Julia–

My Heart has turned to you many many times, though my pen so seldom, for it seems sometimes as if there is a spell upon my writing. When I received Antonio Filicchi's first letter expressing your kind attention to him, while I blessed you for it in my soul, I thought another week shall not pass without repeating to my friend, at least that I am her own Betty Bayley in affection, for fondly as I loved you then, it could not be a comparison with the love of my soul for you now which would give a part of itself, to make you a part of itself. There you dear mad creature is logic, for you the explanation of which is, that I would ever wish you at any expense I could make the purchase to be a partaker in my fanaticism, enthusiasm, anything you may please to call it—To call you back from your delusions and point your views to your next existence [Eternity] before you are called to it. So it is. You think I am in delusion; I know you are in delusion. I ask you, "Julia, where are you going?" You are uncertain. You must either laugh or weep— you cannot reflect on the subject, or pause on it without a sigh. Dear, dear little Soul—Oh that it could see the things that belong to its Peace.

---

[28] Lying-in is a term used in the 19th century referring to childbirth.
[29] 3.27, *Seton Collected Writings,* 1:360.

Write to you once in two months and then only to scold! Patience, dearest, I must let thought take its way at least to you. O how many thoughts crowded on me when I met poor [Colonel Aquila] Giles the other day, forlorn, dejected, shabby, and so changed from what he was—not changed in his kind heart however, for it seemed to feel a convulsion on seeing me and many a reproach for not having done so before. They tell me his fortune is embarrassed and he has a miserable life—Father of Mercies, so goes this World! Let me tell you that in the hope of bettering my property (that is [for] my children), I have entered into an engagement with an English gentleman and his wife[30] (who have failed in their schemes in the interior of our country) to assist them in an English Seminary [which] they are now establishing and which has a prospect of eminent success. My profits are to be a third of whatever this plan produces and includes the education of my children. As I shall have no responsibility or trouble in organizing the plan, I could certainly find no situation more easy, especially as you are to pay the woman I shall employ to mend and to darn [the children's clothing and linen][31]—and when I have a leisure hour, it will be for myself.

My friends, relatives, etc., who have been uniformly cool and composed in relation to all my concerns, are not less so in this instance, but as I shall take care to be distinct in all circumstances of contracts and agreements, I cannot if the worst should happen, be more their dependent than I am now—especially as I have so great a desire, if only to taste a bit of bread of my own earning, if it might be so—but in this I repeat the daily prayer, "Thy will be done."[32]

How are Charlotte and Brother Samuel? Does your dear Maria continue so good and amiable? Is your domestic economy the same? Is your health better? How is the Bachelor? What are you going to do this summer? My heart would rejoice if your jaunt should be this way. In every way and always God bless you, His Peace be with you, as is the sincere affection of Your *E.A.S.*

---

[30] Mr. and Mrs. Patrick White, a Protestant couple.

[31] This is a reference to a previous letter dated March 5, 1805, in which Elizabeth writes about wanting to "procure a person who will rid me of the dreaded burden of patching and darning" in order to devote more time to teaching music and French to her oldest daughter Anna Maria.

[32] Matthew 6:10.

My Darlings are quite well. Anna always speaks of you sweetly, affectionately, "My Aunt Scott." Kate says "she is mine, too." Rebecca is a cherub, but my saucy boys almost master me.

10th July 1805[33]

Dearest Julia,

My heart is by your bedside recalling all the tenderness and affection with which it used to watch and console you. If I had my choice of being by a wish anywhere in the world, that spot I would eagerly fly to. Your friend Mrs. Seaman says you have been very ill, and while I have imagined you enjoying some sweet summer retreat or jaunt of fashion—the poor little head and heart have both been aching and oppressed with suffering. Dear, dear Julia how much I wish to be with you. Tell Maria, I beg it as a mark of affection, that she will write me a line. I hope you will leave the city as soon as possible. Happy I should be if your excursions may lead to me—for although my time is occupied, it would be much more convenient for you to see me now, [than] when you were here last summer. My situation is very comfortable, the family I am with are very friendly, but the school makes no appearance—three scholars added to our 9 children is all.[34] Many are promised in the fall—well, succeed or not succeed, it must be right—my case cannot be worse, nor can it be better for my real enjoyment, than it now is. While I have you, Mrs. [Sarah] Startin, and [Antonio] Filicchi, that is saying a great deal, but it is truly so. Nothing can be worse than a state of dependence, but if it is my allotment, it cannot be better than when supplied by the hand of real friendship.

You would have received a letter from me acknowledging your mark of love received the 18th May, but I have had a succession of trouble—first, in the prospect of losing my sweet Kate with an inflammatory fever;[35] and afterwards with my poor bones wearied out almost refusing to go any more, or if obliged to make the effort, overpowered with faintness and a giddy head. Mrs. Startin has helped very much to restore me with the simple remedy of a glass of wine every day. Now the suffering is nearly past. I wish I could know you were as well. Do beg Maria to write me. Kate is

---

[33] 4.1, *Seton Collected Writings,* 1:380.
[34] The nine children include the five Setons and four of Mr. and Mrs. White.
[35] Kate was five years old at the time.

recovering fast. The other darlings are quite well and my heart loves you most sincerely.

EAS.

Remember me to dear Charlotte and Brother[.] Filicchi offers you his "grateful and respectful compliments."

28th August 1805[36]

When I look at the date of your most affectionate letter, I can scarcely believe that it is not yet answered. I did not receive it though for many days after it was written, owing to my removal at my Brother Post's at Greenwich.[37] Unexpectedly, indeed, it came to me, for the straight story I had had from my blundering [Antonio] Filicchi of your illness, added to the long silence which succeeded the pressing entreaties I had addressed to both yourself and Maria for only one line, led me to imagine the worst. I even dreaded to hear from Philadelphia. Judge then my delight on receiving a letter from your own dear hand.

Two days preceding Quarter day,[38] Mr. [Patrick] White informed me that he had been disappointed in the receipt of money he had expected and could not pay his rent after the present quarter. Consequently the house must be given up to the landlord, and I must be off to prevent his securing my little possessions. [Wright] Post hurried me to his country seat and in a few hours I found myself in a new state of existence, most desirable in many respects, but in some most inconvenient, yet the balance is far on the best side as it respects my health and that of the darlings. I had become so feeble as to be subject to excessive faintness on the least exertion—good Mrs. [Sarah] Startin nursed me with candle and old wine daily, but I believe the change of air was so indispensable that if necessity of one kind had not forced me to it, another would. Although my health is certainly mended here, I am but a shadow, and all my anticipations are pointing to my only Home [in Heaven].

[36] 4.3, *Seton Collected Writings*, 1:383.

[37] Brother-in-law, Dr. Wright Post and his wife Mary Bayley Post, lived in Greenwich Village.

[38] Quarter day probably refers to the end of the financial quarter, June 30.

Dear Emma's death gave me a heavy blow,[39] sitting up with her and seeing her struggles was almost too much. You may well, my love, make the retrospect of what once was, and how is it possible, my dear, dear Julia, you can divest your mind of what must be—Patience—but you must forgive me if I feel unceasing solicitude on this subject. Eternity, my precious friend, is a long, long day. And I have seen so many hurried off with scarce a pause to contemplate the dreadful object, that it is impossible to think of you with the tenderness, which will accompany your image in my soul, without its enquiring with agony, "Is my Julia to be one of those?" Or when the spirit is left to linger in a wasting frame, its powers inactive and saddened with the accumulated infirmities and pains of our Human Nature, how shall it form or progress in the union with the Divine Nature which we are well assured must form the happiness of our future existence—or if permitted—but stop, dear friend, you say, "[I] know all these things." You do know them, my darling, and therefore you resist that Divine Spirit which would then speak Peace to your Soul, and with heavenly consolations sooth every pang of parting nature, while it guided you to the eternal blessings you will so earnestly covet.

I have had the indescribable satisfaction of attending Mrs. [Charlotte Barclay] Bayley in her last hours.[40] I believe I have expressed to you my pleasure in receiving from her, since my return Home, every mark of Peace and reconciliation, which also gives me the double enjoyment of the confidence and affection of the dear girls Helen and Mary Bayley.[41] Their situation is truly melancholy. Indeed I feel more than I can tell for them. Sister Craig's little darling [infant Henry] is all she would have wished and the only comfort of its almost inconsolable father.[42] There is so great an alarm about fever that I feel this may be the last letter you may receive from me for a long while.

Your Anna Maria and sweet Kit are quite well. Anna Maria is with Mary [who is] trying to console and amuse her.[43] They are extremely

[39] Charlotte Amelia (Emma) Bayley Craig died July 22, 1805, at age 26.
[40] Charlotte Barclay Bayley was the second wife of Dr. Richard Bayley and step-mother of Elizabeth Seton.
[41] Helen and Mary Bayley were half-sisters to Elizabeth Bayley Seton.
[42] Henry Craig was Charlotte Amelia (Emma) Bayley Craig's newborn son who survived his mother by only a few months.
[43] Mary Fitch Bayley was the older sister of the deceased Charlotte Amelia (Emma) Bayley Craig.

attached. I hope you will never reproach me for the little use I have as yet made of your goodness to her. I will write you more fully, my dearest friend, when I am able. May God protect and bless you, forever.

Your *EAS.*

ورو

20th November 1805[44]

My dear, dear Julia,

What passes in your dear heart respecting your poor friend? You do not call her ungrateful—forgetful—but rather, consider the most probable cause of her long silence and attribute it to its true reason, a heavy head and heavy heart. Whenever it would address one who has all its affection and confidence—having had nothing but cares and anxieties to communicate to you, either as it related to myself or others, whenever affection suggested [that I] write to Julia, the same affection pleaded, "What, to grieve and pain her?" But now that a Home and Home comforts again are mine,[45] and life and cheerfulness are reanimated, it is sweet to relieve you from the solicitude, which I know my peculiarly hard case must have occasioned in the heart that so truly loves me. It seemed as if there was no escape from the inconveniences and trouble I was necessitated to give the family of my Brother [Wright] Post, the more kind they were to me, the more painful was my sense of it, but according to the old principle by constantly looking up, and reinforcement of patience, the poor Spirit was broken down to bear everything as it happened and prepared with silent resignation for the future, when most unexpectedly Mr. John Wilkes made the proposal of the old scheme of receiving the pupils of Saint Mark's School[46] as Boarders. This plan, so much dreaded before I had drank deep of my cup, was now embraced with eagerness, and I am removed with my Treasures [children] to a very pleasant dwelling two miles from the city and, on Monday next, expect twelve or fourteen children committed to my care to board, wash, and mend for. Your provision for my Anna enables me to pay a good old Woman whom I have known for many years, to take a great part of the burden off me, and to keep my darling companion and comfort at Home,

---

[44] 4.11, *Seton Collected Writings,* 1:395.

[45] Elizabeth and her family moved to Stuyvesant Lane in the Bowery near Saint Mary's Episcopal Church in November 1805.

[46] The school conducted by Rev. William Harris was located at Saint Mark's Church.

98

a Mother's pen must not be trusted to describe what my Anna is to me. Her mind and Intelligence have progressed these last twelve months as much as her loveliness and grace of features.

6th December

My Julia must consider for me how difficult it is to catch even half an hour from my bee hive. We begin at the dawn of day, and by the time all is done, I actually fall asleep even at my prayers. But my heart has been lifted with thanks to God and melts with tenderness inexpressible at the thought of all your love and tenderness to me—tears will start when you say that I have still a place in the heart of Brother Sam [Sitgreaves]. Is it possible that he has so large a share of sorrow, too? Earnestly I pray that it may draw his soul to the Source of Consolation. Oh how pleased I should be to be always near him in our future existence, since in this I have been allowed so small a taste of his dear society—and you, my darling friend, shall we be forever united there? But stop—my eyes are blinded by these questions—and I must now tell you that our sweet, dear little blossom is withered and gone. Our precious little Henry Craig is gone to his Mother.[47] Such is the inscrutable dispensation. His Father is now only a shadow, an image of wretchedness. Mrs. [Eliza] Sadler suffers almost as much. Dear Helen [Bayley Craig] is very much recovered, but scarcely can bear this privation of her little darling.

When you tell me of your exertions and cares, you never say how the little tender frame supports the burden.[48] Dear, dear Julia, much I fear you will not consider how much you try it until it is too late. And will our dear John Scott soon become your protector,[49] your friend, and comfort, too, I trust—which added to Maria's excellent mind and affectionate attentions will, I hope, repay you a part of the indescribable cares and solicitudes you have borne for them. I rejoice that you are so near Charlotte this winter, but do not let the world run too much away with you. Sometimes say, "Julia, where are we going?" I hope this happy season will find you both as happy as it does me, scarcely can that happiness be realized which has given me again a home—three dollars a week for each boy.[50] With washing and mending

---

[47] Charlotte Amelia Bayley Craig died in childbirth in July 1805. Although her son Henry survived, he died four months later.
[48] Elizabeth Seton is asking how her friend Julia Scott copes with the challenges of life.
[49] Julia Scott's son, John (Jack) Morin Scott, became a lawyer.
[50] Elizabeth's boarders who attended Saint Mark's school.

paid for, [it] will help at least to make us less a burden. The pleasure of doing something for my darlings makes every labor easy. They already have their comfortable clothing in anticipation of your love and care. Kit is the gayest little being you can imagine, with a very quick capacity—Rebecca is doted on by us all—the 100 dollars laid by safely—it is a store for necessity—Anna will attend an excellent dancing Master at Mrs. Farquhar's[51] (who is our near neighbor), on the strength of it—not for the steps, but to obtain a little polish and to please Aunt Scott.

This blotted scratching is unpardonable but indeed, dear, I have not time to copy it——

20th January 1806[52]

Every day since the beginning of the year I have thought this Evening I will write to my Julia, but weariness or some interruption has always disappointed me. This season finds me so much more comfortable and happier in every respect than the last, that your dear heart would rejoice if it could witness the change. My food is sweetened with the thought that I do my part to obtain it, and love and gratitude to Him who has ordered it so, that it nourishes and strengthens the poor old body while often the heart so overflows as to communicate its delight to all around it, and the plainest materials form a luxurious feast. Think of me sometimes when your cook does not do her duty. Think of me sometimes when little wasps of vexation beset you. Think of me sometimes when your heart feels the futility of earthly enjoyments and sighs for a possession it can never find here. Then remember that your friend never calls at the Throne of Mercy without pleading for yours, as for her own soul.

Ah Julia, Julia, when that inevitable hour comes, the moments you now give to Him will be the only time remembered with pleasure. When you see the tears of your dear children, you will then feel that you have been only as the Mother of their bodies while the Divine Image in their souls has been disfigured, if not sullied by a mistaken education, which while it fits them for an uncertain and transient existence, leaves them uninstructed or indifferent for the one which must be Eternal. Since you

---

[51] Elizabeth Curzon Farquhar, Elizabeth's aunt by marriage.
[52] 4.13, *Seton Collected Writings*, 1:399.

know it, dearest, and why repeat it—how can I write without showing my heart? How conceal one of its most earnest desires, which is that you will reflect and resolve in time. Lean your head on that dear little white hand. Close your eyes and imagine the present routine of your life past, and your Guardian Spirit introducing you in your future state of existence. Dear, dear soul, it will be no dream. An account must be given, and He who is now our Compassionate Redeemer will then be the inexorable Judge. But the handsome establishment equipages,[53] fashionable friends, decided habits, bent of the mind, etc., etc., etc., etc., etc., are all in the way. Your dear little soul is imprisoned in its body, and both in the world, out of which it cannot be released without many a painful struggle. Never let it enter your mind that you cannot be good in the station you are placed in. On the contrary, that is the very place God has appointed, and a performance of the duties of it would insure your Salvation. The only danger, my darling is, your abuse of it. For to be rich, honorable, and distinguished are all of His appointment, but the giving them the service of the Soul as well as the Body, is contrary to the convictions of your own upright mind, as well as to every principle of a Christian Spirit.

Is the plan the same as formerly? Mother with you? Hitty still happy? Does not Charlotte grow old? Tell me of Maria, of Harriet—dear Brother,[54] and most of all of your dear precious self. Send me a close written letter for a New Year's gift and do tell me all, as if seated by my side. I love to draw a picture when I think of you. Your dear John Scott is then in the character [which] a Mother's heart so fondly anticipates—with every promise of a Friend and Protector pictured in his countenance if it is as when he used to ask "Petchy Pailey"[55] [sic, Betsy Bayley] for a Kiss. Sweet fellow! How I should like to give him a dozen now. Make them think of me, dear, as their true friend.

You asked me long ago about my religious principles. I am gently, quietly, and silently a good Catholic. The rubs, etc., are all past. Well and I kiss my Crucifix, which I have loved for so many years, and say they are only mistaken.

[53] Fancy carriages.

[54] Julia's relatives: Susanna Deshon Sitgreaves, her mother; Mehitabel Cox Markow; Charlotte Sitgreaves Cox; Maria Litchfield Scott; Harriet Sitgreaves, Julia's niece; and Samuel Sitgreaves.

[55] Apparently John Scott was unable to pronounce Betsy Bailey correctly and a childhood lisp made it sound like "Petchy Pailey."

So, we go, dear Julia—travelling on. Take care Miss where you stop—think, you may meet a Tender Father who will say, "my Child was lost and is found. Come Home. Here is rest." But if He should say "I have called, and you would not answer—Go."[56] Think! Think about it. May He bless you, love you, and make you his Own, forever and ever—is the prayer from the Soul of Your,

EASeton.

[Antonio] Filicchi will hand you [this. He has] taken upon himself the expense of my Boys' education and promises them the same situation my [half-]brothers Richard [Bayley] and [Guy] Carleton [Bayley have had] with the friendship he had for their father. This [is a] burden off my mind. They will go to the College[57] immediately, if he can obtain them a situation.

∾❧∾❧∾❧

Sunday Night 12ᵗʰ May 1806[58]

My darling dear Julia,

My heart is almost too happy to write you—my darling boys are on their way to George Town College[59] with Mr. James Barry of Washington City. They may stay a few days in Philadelphia.

The bearer of your last letter must be an odd genius. After delivering it in a moment of great hurry, when I was giving my great family their dinner, he promised to call again, which he did three weeks after on Thursday morning, the only day of the week I go to town. [He] stayed an hour with my old sewing lady, played the piano, and went away before my return, leaving word he would call again. Not having done so, I suppose the affair is finished—as must this handsome scrawl, being greatly, greatly hurried.

Your Own dear *EAS*

Kiss my boys 100 times for me.

∾❧∾❧∾❧

---

[56] Cf. Luke 15:32 and Matthew 22:1-14.

[57] Saint Mary's College in Baltimore, founded and administered by the Society of Saint Sulpice (Sulpicians).

[58] 4.18, *Seton Collected Writings,* 1:407.

[59] Georgetown College was founded in 1789 by Bishop John Carroll.

My dearest, dearest Julianna,

When I would write to you, my heart presents a thousand tender expressions which it dares not utter, and you would scarcely receive with pleasure, as you are quite unconscious of the many combinations which give rise to them. But this, my dear friend, you surely know that your steady unremitting affection in my worldly shipwreck is a sweet consolation, and one of the very few remaining endearments of this life, which added to past remembrances—the idea of Husband and Father, I could lay myself at your dear little feet, and hold them in my bosom.

Are you once more arranged at home? And has not the fatigue exhausted you? No heavy cold—aching head or heavy heart? My Julia, what a toil and how mixed with care and vexation, if the object is attained; but that neither you nor I can alter, while your immediate situation must necessarily create them, your daily occupations and the objects around you unavoidably produce a succession of them, but, Julia dear, you bear the chain and love it, too.

Friday 20th November

My darling Friend, you must write to me. Do not say "She is an Outré[61] creature and cannot enter into my views." She does enter into them, my love, grieves that you are under certain influences which are with so much difficulty controlled, and commits you to God with a tenderness of affection which can be expressed to Him alone.

How is Maria? Our saucy John and your dear little self? Is Mrs. Cox, or rather let me say, dear Charlotte, better from her summer exertions? Are there any consequences? Do you hear from Brother Samuel? Is H's love returned?[62]

How is your personable Friend, as [Andrew Barclay] Bayley calls him? Is Home in the same position as it relates to _____ many, many questions I would ask you—and you who feel so much for my position would ask as many in return—which are answered by simply saying, "as you

---

[60] 4.26, *Seton Collected Writings*, 1:418.
[61] Exaggerated or strange (French).
[62] Elizabeth was inquiring after either Mehitabel "Hitty" Cox or another niece, Harriet Sitgreaves.

left me,"—except that John Wilkes[63] is married, as you probably know. Of course, I am the more interested not to trespass more on his benevolence.

A gentleman of very great respectability from Baltimore, the Superior of the college there has endeavored to interest me in the establishment I have heard you mention, with approbation in Philadelphia.[64] Madam (I do not know who), who keeps the celebrated boarding school, but the aim of my desires if I were to change the present situation is very different, although certainly the idea of going to Philadelphia, or rather to you, would be delightful to me—but no more of that.

Your Anna and Kit are quite well. I have the most consoling accounts from my sweet boys. My strength has, I believe, increased since my favorite season has commenced. Again, I repeat, tell me all you can of [your] little precious self, and love your poor friend, as your own your true friend.

Forever,

EAS

12th January 1807[65]

My darling Julia,

I wrote you five or six weeks ago perhaps more, and do not now remind you with reproach, but with a real apprehension that you may be ill, or that there is some serious reason for so long a silence, which if occasioned by your usual unwillingness to write and the coldness of your dear little fingers, might have been supplied by the warm heart of your gallant Jack[66] who I know would willingly relieve anxiety in any one, and readily in his old

---

⁶⁴ Rev. Louis William Dubourg was president of Saint Mary's College, Baltimore, which he had founded in 1799 as a preparatory academy or boarding school for boys adjacent to Saint Mary's Seminary, established in 1791.

⁶⁵ 4.29, *Seton Collected Writings,* 1:425.

⁶⁶ John Morin Scott, the son of Lewis Allaire and Julianna Sitgreaves Scott, moved to Philadelphia with his mother after the death of his father in 1798. He was educated there and at Princeton after which he practiced law and served several terms in the Pennsylvania House of Representatives. He married Mary Emelen May 15, 1817, the daughter of George and Sarah Fishbourne Emelen, a prominent Quaker family. John and Mary Emelen Scott had seven children.

friend. Tell him I challenge him in prose or verse, short or long, any measure that will assure me you are well.

I am unusually well this winter, quite contented with the necessity of the case, sometimes doubtful though as it respects my darlings whether it is not a duty to take them from the influence of my rude and unmannered inmates[67]—but God will direct. Anna is almost as much a woman as her Mother and much more discreet, and considerate—Your Kate is a treasure of amiable disposition and promising talents. My sweet sister[68] rewards my former attention to her by every assistance in her power for their instruction. We are all prospering dear, except poor Bayley[69] who is hugging the hope of his little arm—full with a heart discontent and quite uncertain of his future prospects. How much happier is his "poor Sis" whom he so much pities. Looking up steadily spares the pains, both of retrospection and anticipation, but, on my part, I greatly pity him, as I, having been behind the curtain of all this sweet happiness he looks for so naturally, certainly have a very different opinion of it from that his imagination so warmly pictures. You, my darling, if you had the job to do again would also, I believe, take it rather gently.

How is my brother Sam?[70] I suppose he has come to his senses, or rather his right senses, before this time. My dearest, best, and oldest, strongest love to him when you have the opportunity. I have many fears for the health of dear Charlotte [Cox] this winter; and if not sure that any sorrow pressing on your heart would have induced you the more readily to write me, should have been apprehensive [that] her complaints had increased.

Will you be pleased to tell me if your personable friend is still your *humble servant*, or if you are any nearer in the sense of Saint Paul to

---

[67] Elizabeth's boarders who attended Saint Mark's school.

[68] Elizabeth's youngest sister-in-law, Cecilia Seton, was helping with school lessons for the Seton children while she was living with them.

[69] Elizabeth was possibly referring to her half-brother, Andrew Barclay Bayley and his management of his inheritance or to his courtship of Harriet Seton, Elizabeth's sister-in-law.

[70] Samuel Sitgreaves, the son of William and Susanna Deshon Sitgreaves and a brother of Julia Sitgreaves Scott, as a lawyer in Easton, Pennsylvania. From 1794 to 1798 he served as a member of the House of Representatives and from 1798 to 1802 as a commissioner representing the United States government in England. He married Mary Kemper.

becoming his [wife].[71] O do, dear Julia, write me if but in short hand—my best and tenderest love are always yours.

EAS.

Remember me to dear Maria—and to Harriet.[72]

❧❧❧❧❧

10th April 1807[73]

My much loved Julia,

If you are not out of patience with your friend. It is much more than I deserve, as it is not probable that you are acquainted with the melancholy reason of my long silence, which really has been unavoidable. You will say so, when you know that for several weeks now, and sometimes three nights of the week, I have been obliged to sit up and watch the dying hours of our poor Eliza Maitland.[74] You know, love, that persons in sickness and pain wish for the presence of those who are experienced in them, and this poor Sister found, or thought she found more comfort in my nursing, than in the attention of anyone else. You may be sure in such a moment I could not add a pain to the dear parting Soul, and—

One more added to my list of agonies—she has left five as helpless little beings as ever wanted a Mother's care. Their father[75] is an unfortunate man, and the family will take charge of them—poor little lambs——

Julia, my precious Friend—this dear Eliza did not love the world; she had a bitter portion in it, and you would say a life passed in the slavery of poverty and secluded from those allurements which commonly endear us to the present scene would have ensured her at least a peaceful death—some nights before her last, in an interval of ease, she conversed with me and observed herself that such had been her situation, but added: "How is it that until we are just going, we never think of the necessary dispositions to meet death?" I made some consolatory reflections to her, but although she said but little on the subject during her illness, which was long and painful, and her mind naturally quite uninterested in it, her fears and dread

---

[71] Elizabeth was asking Julia if she planned to get married. Cf. EPH 5:22.

[72] Julia's niece.

[73] 4.33, *Seton Collected Writings,* 1:434.

[74] The wife of James Maitland, Eliza Seton Maitland, was a sister-in-law to Elizabeth Seton.

[75] James Maitland, Elizabeth's brother-in-law, had been involved in Seton, Maitland and Company which suffered bankruptcy.

continued to the last. Oh Julia, Julia, Julia—"the last last last sad silence!" The soul departing without Hope, its views, its interests centered in a world it is hurried from. No Father's sheltering arms—No heavenly home of joy— My Julia, Julia, Julia—Eternity—a word of transport or of Agony—Your Friend, your own, your true, your dear friend, begs you, supplicates you in the Name of God—think of IT. O if she should see your precious soul torn, dragged, an unwilling Victim—what a thought of horror.

15th April

Do not be angry with me, dearest Friend. Say not the entreaty is from a heart torn with misfortune or depressed by melancholy—not so— never was a more cheerful or contented heart than your friend's—absolutely reposed in the bosom of the tenderest of Fathers.[76]

How I wish I was near you I would sing and laugh for you, my darling Julia, and show you how sweet, how very sweet, it is to look over the hills that surround our Valley—and then you know as we are, both past thirty, we might form some plans between this and sixty. The truth is that I have never felt myself bound to my dear little Sister Post,[77] at any time half as much [as at present]. Although often two weeks together elapse without our having the least communication, yet except some plan occurred of certain advantage, I must jog on, and rest quiet in the certainty of encountering difficulties in every allotment, and let the current take its course. He who sits above smiles at the anxious calculating heart, and makes everything easy to the simple and confiding. I may well act upon this plan having found it to be the only source of real Peace.

No doubt, poor Harriet [Sitgreaves][78] is signed and sealed before this—and perhaps gone—dear child. The beauteous vision will vanish, but it is all in the course of things. May God protect and bless her! Is your dear Maria improved by her visit? What strange recollections the name of Caton give rise to in my silly fancy.[79] I could laugh like a fool even with myself at the remembrance of an evening Mrs. Caton passed with us in Wall

---

[76] God the Father.

[77] Mary Bayley Post was older than Elizabeth, so this is probably a reference to Mary as petite.

[78] Julia's niece.

[79] Possibly Mary (Polly) Carroll Caton (1770-1846) , who was the daughter of Charles Carroll of Carrollton and niece of Archbishop John Carroll. She married Richard Caton in 1786 and they were the parents of Emily, Louisa, and Mary Caton who later attended Saint Joseph's Academy, Emmitsburg, Maryland.

Street.[80] She was one of My William's[81] favorites and my friends the Barrys are attached to her. Therefore I say to folly, Hush.

I cannot tell you, dear Julia, how your generous attention presses on my heart and when your letter containing the remittance comes, the comparative view will present itself—as certainly, it is not the plan of Brother Post[82] that we should receive the sum subscribed, except if there was more necessity than the present. You await neither calculations nor receipts but the expanded heart flies before all. The dear children you love most, promise most—Anna is a piece of harmony in mind and person, both; Kit has a most amiable disposition with very superior abilities.

Will you tell dear Lott I love her dearly, and wait in anxious expectation of the NEWS.[83] Surely she will not be contented with one pair.

I suppose Brother [Samuel Sitgreaves] has an army [of children] by this time—may prosperity attend Him. How dearly, dearly I should love to have a peeping corner among you all. I guess I should see queer things. Remember me to your dear ones—think of me—love me—take care of yourself! Go on your dear little knees before you put away this letter and lift up your heart [to God]—Adieu.

Love ever yours *EAS*

෨෴෨෴෨෴

22nd April 1807[84]

If I did not feel my heart full and overflowing with tenderest, truest love to my Julia, I should be sure it was no longer in my bosom—dear dear Friend, can it be that I have so faithful, so dear a heart, still left from the wreck of past blessings—while mine retains one throb of life it cannot forget to love you.

Your Dr.[85] I believe borrowed a look and smile from you—or at least the sight of him recalled your smile of mischief, so strongly to my fancy, that I could not retain the character or personify the stranger to him. You

---

[80] The Setons formerly lived at 27 Wall Street in lower Manhattan in New York City.
[81] William Magee Seton, Elizabeth's deceased husband.
[82] Dr. Wright Post, brother-in-law of Elizabeth Seton.
[83] Charlotte Sitgreaves Cox had given birth to twins.
[84] 4.34, *Seton Collected Writings*, 1:437.
[85] Dr. Bollman was the bearer of this letter.

know that *in facto* your friend is never that to any one—the heart flies out so quickly—but it is time to be circumspect, and sometime at least to behave, but never mind, it must go in the course of things—

On Saturday last the 18th my long looked for reply to you was put in the post. I have observed that Mrs. [Sarah] Startin (who is not more regular in her affairs, etc., than your dear little self) always requires of me a receipt for whatever money I receive from her, in order to keep her books correct, and told me that I should enclose yours without any question—but as I do not know how to date the beginning of your remittances, you must direct it yourself, dear friend.

My precious merry little Cis[86] is gone, and I may truly say, I am lost. Anna's disposition is so different. She knows how to put her cheek to mine and mix a silent tear, but to turn that tear to a smile is only the province of sweet Celia.[87] Mrs. [James] Seton's confinement[88] which has lately taken place separates us now—for how long I know not. She has the power and disposition to make herself so useful to them that most probably we shall be separated.

Eliza Farquhar[89] is going fast to heaven—with the most angelic dispositions that [I] ever met in a being so circumstanced, I believe—Consumption.

—Patience—turn and turn, about as the children say.

Good Night, dear Julia, dear—My love to your darlings—the book will be a great acquisition to my sweet girl[90] who really improves in everything and has no fault so dangerous as her loveliness. Tell your saucy John how much I thank him. Farewell, farewell, ever ever

yours *Ɛ A.S.*

Thursday night–

ও৶৶৶৶৶

---

[86] Her youngest sister-in-law, Cecilia Seton.

[87] Cecilia Seton, Elizabeth's youngest sister-in-law, had returned to James Seton's household.

[88] Mary Gillon Hoffman Seton was the wife of James Seton. Confinement is a term used in the nineteenth century referring to the final stage of pregnancy.

[89] Eliza "Zide" Farquhar was a cousin of the Setons.

[90] Anna Maria Seton.

My darling Julia,

How is it that strong minds, weak minds, and all sorts of minds, I believe, are subject to melancholy and unaccountable forebodings often without being able either to trace their source or resist their impressions? Scarcely more than one day's journey separates us, Yet, like a fool, fancy often pictures you suffering in mind or body, and certainly in all events, sighing and wearied, with real or ideal evils which are, and ever must be, the certain attendants of a life which seeks its pleasures everywhere but from within.

Affection, fervent, anxious affection would make enquiries, but the pen drops on the reflection, "dear little Soul it is a pain to her to write— she has a thousand occupations"—and indeed sometimes I am so sure you will again take the fashionable route that I expect to hear you are in town from day to day. Anna often has said, "I do believe there is Aunt Scott's carriage!"

The most painful, cruelly painful circumstance and circumstances of poor Mary Seton's[92] death (Mrs. James Seton) has been more sensibly felt by myself (tho' apparently the person least interested) than can be imagined, and once more completely covered—every power and faculty of my mind with the veil of sorrow—so many painful combinations never before united in the death of any one of the many I have been so nearly connected with— nor deprived my soul of those cheering, consoling reflections which have always accompanied its deepest afflictions—but as in every other instance now, too, I look up in silent acquiescence adoring that Dear Hand which will one day show every apparently dark and mysterious event in the most beautiful and perfect perspective of wisdom and harmony. The much loved darling Cecilia, by this sudden change, is removed from me. Her poor brother [James Seton] finds his greatest consolation in her faithful and unwearied attentions to himself and his children (he has 8—five girls).[93] Therefore my deprivation is easily reconciled having many comforts [which] he has not.

---

[91] 4.43, *Seton Collected Writings,* 1:450.

[92] Mary Gillon Hoffman Seton, Elizabeth's sister-in-law, had died in June probably as a result of childbirth.

[93] Cecilia Seton, who would be fifteen in August, cared for the children who had just lost their mother.

Mrs. [Eliza] Sadler and Mrs. [Catherine] Dupleix are on the point of embarking for Ireland. Sister Post is at her summer residence on Long Island. My dear Barrys at the Springs; Mrs. [Sarah] Startin at Brunswick. I can lay my hand sweetly on my heart, look up to God and say I am ALONE with you, dear Lord, and my little children.

4th August

My dearest Friend—Your letter of 28th July was sent to me this afternoon by one of my neighbors. How long Brother Post has had it, I know not. It is a great relief to me although you have evidently very little of the sweet peace your friend wishes for you as the choicest gift of Heaven—poor darling Julia—in how many ways you must be tormented. The widow's friend would indeed have gloried in chastising the rascal who usurps your right—surely the fear of being hooted at might have hindered so dishonorable an action; it rouses my Bayley blood. How glad I am Brother will make your cause his own.

You say nothing of your health in the battle. When will the letter come which you promise shall tell me of your dear children? A gentleman mentioned that dear Maria had been in New York on her way to the Springs with Mrs. Somebody, is it so? Is our Trojan John the same? No views of Europe in his head? Our dear Charlotte must have felt the parental pang most keenly—but He knows best—

Everybody is talking of war[94] here and it has seemed impossible for me to feel an interest in the subject, supposing it one of the *Whirlgigs* of our changeable existence which would not be permitted to produce Good or Evil but in subservience to the great plan. Your letter has awakened now the most solicitous desire as if Julia, who is so small a speck, was indeed the whole world to me—or as if the same All Directing Providence would not shelter her in that hour, as in the present—it will—the promise is sure.

Your continued remittance, which I am no more in want of than the great Mogul, is now a real pain to me. Did I want it, I would fly to you sooner than any earthly resource I have—but not in the least want, obliged indeed to put it at interest while I am persuaded the multiplicity of demands on you must make the command of ready money often difficult. I would beg you, dearest friend, at least to suspend it. I have All and more than I want. [Antonio] Filicchi pays the whole of my boys' expenses and 200

---

[94] This was the era of the Napoleonic Wars.

dollars besides. The [John] Wilke's signature goes to my house rent and 300 dollars a year from my inmates.[95] Judge then if I have not more than I want. Mrs. Startin has given once a hundred dollars; Post is silent.

The greatest difficulty I have to encounter is the loveliness of my Anna; she is indeed a being formed to please—Patience—must take it coolly.[96] Little Kit is every day more knit in her Mother's affections. She learns without any of the laboring up hill so common to children. Everything she does is with ease and sweetness, and a little smile of love [is] the only reply to the most difficult task that can be given her. Her assiduity is often a strong contrast to poor Anna's indifference. Nature's plants are indeed various. Rebecca reads and sews without any other instruction than being present at the lessons of her sisters. The boys are said to be the most docile and obedient of all their companions. Bishop [John] Carroll writes me [that] they are extremely beloved and progressing very fast. See how many good things I have to tell you.

Poor Bayley has gone to sea again, half distracted—without prospect or view, but to try for his daily bread—his beloved is an amiable little creature, and her situation truly interesting.[97]

You do not say anything of brother's progeny. Do they multiply? Is his health [good]? I suppose he has long since numbered me among the lunatics—therefore [give] him my hair-brained affection in its primitive warmth. I met a very personable man in the street the other day who I could have vowed was himself, and like to have fallen on his neck—it would have been a fine business to be sure!

Poor Harriet![98] The sigh involuntarily rises at the thought of her— her fate however may (if she has chosen a generous heart for a partner) be eventually more happy than Mrs. Markow's[99] surrounded by her relatives.

When will Maria complete the picture? How different her character must be from either of her cousins, and I am well persuaded will require many more ingredients to form her happiness.

---

[95] Elizabeth's boarders who attended Saint Mark's school.

[96] Her oldest daughter Anna Maria had just turned twelve.

[97] Andrew Barclay Bayley, Elizabeth Seton's younger half-brother, was in love with Harriet Seton, her sister-in-law, and was engaged to marry.

[98] Julia's niece.

[99] Mehitabel Cox Markow, Julia's niece.

Are you in retirement, or only at the distance convenient for visitors, dear, dear Julia? How I should love to be near you in some hidden situation, humble and neat, where I could catch your hour of leisure—not scold you, but console and cheer your dear heart. Sometimes when you are in haste, softly whisper. "Julia, where are you going?" Hush, hush—peace to you, love forever Yours—

You see this letter was to have gone to you 2 weeks ago. The person who was to take it disappointed, or rather, I missed the opportunity—and procrastination, our sympathetic complaint, finished only the first page—the recipe was simply 10 drops of Laudanum, one or 2 of Oil Peppermint, according to its strength, to an ounce vial of water sweetened—

29th November 1807[100]

My dearest Julia–

From some mistake of Brother Post I did not receive your letter until this Morning. The tenderness and affection it repeats is most consoling and grateful, and effectually reproves my silence tho really it would have been most difficult to express my heart within the last three months, and more difficult to suppress to you its inquietude and embarrassment. Somehow or somehow (as Betty Bayley used to say) inquietude knocks long at my door without admittance, or if she surprises me, she finds no room for her restless disposition. In other words, Dear, your friend, is so tired she can rest even upon thorns—tired of contradictions most completely. This is the Prologue, my love, and the comedy is that the parents of my young boarders, who were ten in number, have expressed much dissatisfaction at the liberty their children enjoy in my family and have roasted me handsomely for not keeping them in better order—to which civility I could only reply that the business had been misunderstood, as I supposed my only responsibility was the care of their clothing, food, and a comfortable home. However tho' I tried to laugh it off and pretended not to believe they were in earnest, I have lost three, which is a large drawback in my income, which at best was three hundred dollars short of my expenditure. Let it go round. I can but decamp. You know my encumbrances are not weighty. Sometimes the thought of Philadelphia cheers the scene, but at others the whole heart flies upwards and I would not give a sigh for anything in the interval. Peace,

[100] 4.60, *Seton Collected Writings*, 1:487.

my dear sober friend says, we will jog up the hill as quietly as possible and when the flies and mosquitoes bite, wrap the cloak round and never mind them, they can only penetrate the surface. Darling Julia, how I wish you would buy such a cloak.[101] It costs a good deal at first but it wears so well, and is so comfortable, that it is really worth twice the sum, and—but you can imagine its convenience—the only difficulty is that it is not in fashion. I know I sometimes look shabby enough in mine. The little sheet [of paper] grows short (good Irish). I must leave a large space to thank you for the interesting particulars of your letter which gives me some actual idea of your dear ones as they are.

8th December—

My friend thinks as usual, and justly, too, that she has bestowed her affectionate kindness on an unworthy and careless creature. Every morning and every evening, it has been part of the plan to dismiss this shabby little scrawl, and here it still is—stormy weather, wet walking, a stiff neck, work upon work. How sweet it is to hear from yourself that you have an unusual share of health, that vexations at least are not increased. You never speak of one person who has the power of diminishing or adding essentially to your comfort, if she still resides with you. How I should delight in passing twenty-four hours with you—but—a prisoner, I sigh—yet in dearest company. My dear ones are at the different ages productive of hope rather than the anxiety yours must excite. Anna is making rapid progress in her music. She often plays off simply what I am obliged to study. You talk of taking her from me. Dearest friend, if it was difficult two years ago—imagine now—softly, softly my heart. Hereafter we may wish what now we pronounce impossible. My fate, Julia, is as uncertain as the world we are thrown upon—Patience—look to the clouds.

Your bills, my kindest friend, are safe. I am always unwilling to change them, when I do it is for comfort. Three hundred and fifty dollars for this house per annum, three dollars for every load [of] wood put up, four dollars per week for bread. What an extravagance to meet 13 hundred dollars income—and maintain nine young giants besides our little selves. Patience—if they will but allow Peace. At best, it must be such as I used to find in my cabin during a storm. Adieu. Adieu. Adieu.

May the best of blessings be yours forever **MEAS**

---

[101] For a time Elizabeth attempted to interest Julia in becoming a Catholic.

Stuyvesant's lane, Bowery, near Saint Mark's Church. Two white houses joined, left hand—[102] children the sign of the dwelling—no number. Well dearest, are you wiser? How I shall rejoice in that day you give this direction to your coachman.[103]

12th December

Anna [has] an ulcerated sore throat—Kit [is] sick—[my] sweet little self [is] wearied, faint and good for nothing. The little letter remained in the secretary for want of a carrier to town where I have been only once since I received yours. Do not be angry with me; indeed you must forgive.

January 16th 1808[104]

My dear darling Julia,

My heart has flown to your little bosom a hundred times since this year began; it would wish there to read what perchance may not be written—to see if the sweet character of peace and content are plainly inscribed, if the little corner so long occupied by your poor hair-brained friend is undisturbed by the bustle and intrusions of the day. It is at the hours of midnight when see-sawing the chair and humming to my poor darlings, I have thought of you most. For several weeks an ulcerated sore throat has had possession of us alternately, as soon as one recovered another was seized, until it had made the round—but we are all recovered and merry again—as it was an epidemic we had it all to ourselves, so much the better.

I have met with a very serious loss in the death of Mr. James Barry, whom I believe I told you sought me out with his dear wife and presented themselves, entire strangers, solely for the love he had had for my Seton[105]—a plea which at once opened my whole heart to them. From that hour they have shown me and my darlings the most uniform unwearied affection I have ever known except that so precious from my Julia. Miss [Ann] Barry[106] is in a decline and her mother will take her

---

[102] Elizabeth's current address.

[103] Give this direction refers to the address of the Seton's residence.

[104] 4.63, *Seton Collected Writings,* 1:492.

[105] William Magee Seton, Elizabeth's deceased husband.

[106] Ann Barry, called Nancy, was the daughter of James and Joanna Barry, Catholic friends of Elizabeth Seton in New York.

[on] a voyage as soon as this cruel embargo is raised. Then adieu to every inducement to go to town independent of Saint Peters [Church].

Sister and Helen [Bayley][107] (who is thought among the sweetest and handsomest girls in New York) have become votaries of fashion—they are very much in public and Sister Post makes every sacrifice to make her happy. I know it will please you to know this.

And your dear I in the corner is not more molested by the bountiful gentlemen who have left me and my young gentlemen to manage each other—how long I know not. Their school Master is much terrified at the idea of war;[108] they have no idea of his remaining if it takes place. Are you agitated with the rest of the world on the subject? Your last letter expressed some uneasiness. My poor brother-in-law James [Seton] has once more to begin the world again with his eight children. How the poor Setons are melted down—but he bears it as a man and is universally respected and pitied. Cecilia [Seton], he says, is his greatest comfort, her health is greatly mended.

Will you please, my dear Mrs. Glorianna,[109] to send me a few lines to let me know that you are well and hope that I'm the same. Do. Do. Do for pity's sake.

Give John Scott a New Year smack for me and tell him I hope he may live until he is wedded to wisdom which, I believe, will require an extension of time quite equal to his wishes—saucy Mrs. Seton. Remember me to dearest Maria tenderly, affectionately and offer Mrs. Charlotte the "glowing fervor" of my Bayley-Heart. Bless you forever.

Your *EAS.*

My sweet Kit and Rebecca send you messages of love when they find I am writing Aunt Scott. Anna Maria is at James Seton's for some days.

---

[107] Mary Bayley Post and Helen Bayley, Elizabeth's sister and half-sister.
[108] Rev. William Harris was troubled by the continuing European conflicts.
[109] An affectionate name for Julia Scott. Glorianna is also the name of the Faerie Queen in *The Faerie Queen* by Edmund Spencer. Elizabeth was probably familiar with this famous allegorical epic containing themes related to virtue.

My Friend—my dear, dear Julia—

Can it be your letter is so long unanswered, tho my heart made so warm a reply on its first reception—and never thinks of you without a thousand emotions of affection, gratitude, and tenderest remembrances. How often these thoughts arise you would scarcely believe from the nature of my occupations—except you could know the force of those affections, which so many years have riveted to you, independent of your unremitted and precious friendship. Let my Julia feel one consolation in the changing scene that surrounds her. You have a friend who would fly to you from any part of the world, leave children everything, on the smallest intimation she could be useful to you. I would think the distance between us but a speck if I might hold your dear head when it ached or banish one hour of sorrow—that dear All Ruling Hand which has granted me so many favors will, I trust, hear my earnest prayer that I may one day be able to prove to you how true, how heartfelt my attachment is. Of all the many attachments I have had, you are the only one on earth who my heart turns to in the simple unrepressed warmth of confiding love—every other is shackled with hesitations, doubts, calculations, etc., so contradictory to my nature. What is all the world to one who bears no part in it but the charge of five innocent docile children.

Your Anna Maria's progress in music is uncommon for her age and every new lesson she excels in pictures to me the delight they who are gone would have had in hearing her. The only check to these regrets is the anticipation of the pleasure she may in a future period afford to my Julia. She is very neat at her needle and pen, and translates French with facility and pleasure, her lessons of geography are limited to Turner and Morse[111] which is as much as is necessary for a general idea of it. She is fond of occupation, but like her poor Mother, only attached to reading and writing. Her strength and health would delight you and that reserved, quiet manner (the result of natural temper) saves her from a thousand difficulties I encountered at

---

[110] 4.67, *Seton Collected Writings,* 1:497.

[111] Jedidiah Morse, "father of American geography," was the author of *Geography Made Easy* (1784) and *American Geography* (1789) which were distributed widely. The descriptions by Captain Samuel Turner of his travels in Asia, particularly Tibet, are included.

her age—yet there never was a wilder romp when she meets her favorite companions her Aunt Celia and Emma Seton (James eldest daughter).

Sweet Kate who forms every action and thought from the eyes and words of her Mother is a different disposition—always in earnest, diligent in everything she thinks may please, every heart leans towards her—mine, too much, because her health is very delicate. How can I write you dearest always of these darlings—who or what else can I speak of—for weeks together I see no one else—the dear interesting family of the Barrys to whom I was indebted for so much comfort and unceasing attention are gone—the Father to Heaven (for he was very, very good), the only dear daughter [Ann] quickly following, is now with her excellent Mother on their way to Madeira in hopes of benefit from a sea voyage.

Your account of Charlotte grieves me—dear amiable Being—may she be happy in life or Death—Harriet's[112] fate awakens many melancholy ideas Parental care and love cherishes uncertain Hope indeed—sweet Sister Helen[113] is engaged to marry a Mr. Kerney of independent fortune, which is the only particular I have yet heard of him, nor have I seen him but hope he will supply to her the many ties she has lost. Her sweet and interesting manner promises everything, but Oh dear Julia what a faithless prospect is that she now contemplates—

Poor [Colonel] Giles stopped me in the street about five minutes but in that time said a volume about your not being yet married, his surprise that you were not, his doubts if you ever would consent to it, etc., etc., etc., etc.—which I answered with a positive assurance you never would be—and who gave me this assurance? Well at least it seemed to brighten the poor soul who looks as if he lived in a ditch. His Madame is sick—unfortunate beings—most truly unfortunate.

How are Maria's ideas directed, to the glittering, or solid views of life? I think she must have too much discernment to be led by a meteor. Yet, at her age we could not even wish her to be correct in her estimate.[114]

Dear, dear, dear Julia, let us love while we live at least. A thousand blessings be with you. Remember me to Brother Sam and dear John when

---

[112] Either Elizabeth's sister-in-law or Julia's niece, both of whom are named Harriet.

[113] Helen Bayley, Elizabeth's half-sister. It is not known whether she married Mr. Kerney. She later married Samuel Craig in 1814.

[114] Maria Scott was 18 years of age.

you write them. Tell dear Charlotte [Cox] I wish my spirit could be infused in some of her remedies and they would soon very soon relieve her. Never will I forget the charm of a day I once passed with her in her chamber—her tears of pain and smile of affection—gone gone forever.

You find the paper is larger—the note is not changed but carefully put by, destined to fulfill on some future day a fervent wish of my heart. Dearest friend, how many of its desires you have enabled it to indulge.

always yours most affectionately

EASeton

March 20—I have been sick, dear friend, or this would have been forwarded many days ago.

23rd April 1808[115]

How well you know the heart of your own friend, my Julia, when you bade me pause and ponder on the flattering question it proposed. You find how patiently I have awaited the discreet moment, but I assure you not from any hesitation in replying to it. One of Brother's children, a piece of himself, his darling, given to my arms and heart.[116] Oh! The crazy brain turns at the thought—but my dearest, my dwelling of 350 dollars rent is exchanged for one of 150,[117] which tho' very convenient and in the street on a line with the one we are in, yet obliges me to contract my personal accommodations. We are five in a room and closet, which might be disagreeable to you in placing the darling.

The boys who remain with me are only five—they leave me as they prepare for college, and my means are much diminished. Yet, as they never afforded me any other advantage than daily bread, neither paying house rent nor fuel, I have not much to regret. So sweet is the Providence that overrules us! At this very moment of solicitude for our destination when

---

[115] 4.73, *Seton Collected Writings*, 1:506.
[116] Apparently Julia proposed to send one of Samuel Sitgreaves' children to board with Elizabeth.
[117] Elizabeth had moved or was about to move to a smaller and less expensive house on the same street.

the present means fails, Mr. Dubourg[118] the President of Saint Mary's College in Baltimore, to whom I communicated my dilemma, has offered to give me a formal grant of a lot of ground situated close to the college, which is out of the town and in a very healthy situation, and procure me immediately the charge of a half-dozen girls (and as many more as I can manage). Added to this, he will take my boys in the college, and the entire charge of them, for a very small consideration in order that [Antonio] Filicchi's money may assist me in another way. Much as this offer delighted me, I urged my want of talents etc. He assures me that Madame La Combe[119] whom he established in a much more unfavorable footing has now more than one hundred young persons in charge of the first families.

Do you shake your dear head, or is the smile of pleasure predominant? How much I wish to know. Do write me as soon as you can. As yet I have not consulted my Brother Post or Mr. [John] Wilkes, but I am sure they foresee the burden we shall be to them when this present living is over, and [they] will readily approve. Yet much must depend on procuring, if possible, the money my Uncle [Dr. John] Charlton[120] left me [so] that a house may be provided on my lot, dearest, and the affair so managed that it may be secured to the children. Unfortunately I did not go at the proper moment and can neither see my Brother nor Mr. Wilkes, but next week we must conclude on something.

Filicchi left me an unlimited credit on *John Murray & Sons* but it will not do to abuse their kindness.[121] The four hundred dollars per annum is already a great deal. We will see—it will all be right. Perhaps God may deny my wish of being so near my darling boys for some good purpose. But, indeed, the thought of joining them gives a strength and courage to my soul which bears it over every impediment.

And now to speak of your dearest self. There is a passage of your letter which would excite the attention of a heart much less attached to you than mine. "Poor girl she knows not how soon, etc." You have told me a war

[118] Rev. Louis William Dubourg, S.S., had first broached this subject to Elizabeth in a general way in November 1806. It was not until April 1808 that Dubourg presented this concrete plan involving Baltimore.

[119] Madame Marie La Combe operated a school for young ladies in Baltimore.

[120] Elizabeth's uncle and benefactor. According to the terms of his will, both Mary Bayley Post and Elizabeth Bayley Seton were to receive $2,500, but this did not happen.

[121] John Murray & Sons of New York handled the Filicchi accounts in the United States. Antonio Filicchi had directed Mr. Murray to disburse funds to Mrs. Seton at her request.

would derange your plans, it is true, but surely your melancholy expression indicates more than a mere lessening of property which, as it would affect the general state of affairs as much as your own, would never deprive my dear Julia's family of the distinction they have ever held. What is it dear, dear friend? How I long to see you and know your whole heart. That dear and virtuous child will never give you pain, therefore your words are mysterious. How soon will you write? Do, do, dear Julia, and of all things, tell me of yourself, of your health, spirits, everything.

Is there any news of Harriet? And dear Charlotte[122] is she better? Her ill health must be a great deprivation to you both. Are there any more pairs [twins] on the way? Dear, dear Charlotte! Offer my tenderest remembrances to your interesting amiable Maria—her friend you speak of is said to be very beautiful etc., and saucy-box came home to see her—no doubt he has a good taste. Maria's friendship is a solid recommendation. I wish his studies may proceed with the same facility as before. Tell the dear fellow he has the best wishes of his ancient sweetheart.

Sunday Evening

My dearest, I must either close this now, or it may be long delayed. A thousand Blessings, be with you –

Your EAS.

1st June 1808[123]

My darling Julia,

Your letter should have been answered by return of the post. Had I not been daily expecting to communicate the final decision of Mr. [John] Wilkes and my Brother Post respecting my removal to Baltimore. That decision is now obtained and with it the most cordial desire of forwarding my plan there, and a pressing advice for my immediate departure, as at this season, the house I occupy may be easily let, and a convenient one can now be procured for me in the vicinity of the college at Baltimore[124] which is out of the city. In short, the time, day, and manner of our departure would have

---

[122] Julia's niece Harriet and Charlotte Sitgreaves Cox, Julia's sister, who had given birth to twins.
[123] 4.74, *Seton Collected Writings,* 1:508.
[124] Saint Mary's College, directed by Rev. Louis William Dubourg, S.S.

been concluded on this very morning, had I not expressed an earnest wish to hear first from you. Therefore, do, if only in ten lines by return of post, tell me how you are circumstanced. Are you yet in affliction? Is your poor Mother worse or better? Could the presence of your own friend relieve you from a moment's sorrow? On your answer depends either my going round by sea, or coming to you in two or three weeks by land.[125] Be sincere in your statement, as they tell me it will be much less expense to go by water. I know so many of us must be an embarrassment to you. Certainly I shall not indulge my wish of seeing you unless the foregoing questions receive an affirmative.

In pain, weariness, and haste, I am

Your Own Friend

EAS

စ်လ်စ်လ်စ်လ်

4th July 1808[126]

My dear, dear Friend,

How often you must have looked for a letter from me since my last; but indeed it has been next to impossible to write. After our arrival here, I went immediately to Washington for my dear boys, and having my family to settle, house to arrange, clothes to repair, and such heat to support as was almost insupportable, it has really been very difficult to write even a line. And oh how much, my dear Julia, may have suffered during this interval. What would I not give to know your exact position. Still I am not yet so engaged but that at the general vacation of August I might come to you, if you even wished it. I scarcely know how to restrain myself, or ask you a question on the subject. Do, do write me, dearest, and say if seeing your poor friend would console you a moment. My house is so near the Seminary and every person so interested to make us happy that an arrangement might easily be made without difficulty as it respects the children. I may accompany our Mrs. [Mary Ann] Barry, or in other words, I should not mind any difficulty which would enable me to express my affection for you, to whom I owe so much. How can I ask you any questions about your Mother, but Julia you must write, if but ten lines.

---

[125] In fact Elizabeth did travel by sea and did not see Julia Scott on her trip to Baltimore.
[126] 5.3, *Seton Collected Writings*, 2:13.

You would scarcely believe the change I experience in my manner of life since I am in my new home. After so long a period of trouble and confusion, to lead a life of regularity and comparative repose—accustomed to find recreation and amusement only in my books, and considering every visitor a thief upon my few, precious moments and almost an intruder, my poor heart was wrapped up in its own solicitudes, or indifferent to every temporal object. But such is the contrast of my present situation, I scarcely dare think of it. We were received by each of the Reverend Gentlemen [Sulpician priests] of the Seminary as their adopted charge. Mr. Dubourg's sister [Victoire D. Fournier] who conducts the regulations of the establishment is a most amiable affectionate character and, tho' beyond forty, a very elegant woman. She arranges my affairs for me such as clothing my dear boys, placing and providing necessary furniture, provisions, etc., etc., with an ease and gaiety of manner, as if the favor was all on my side. I have the advantage of procuring everything I use from the seminary, which as they engage [purchase] by the gross, makes a difference of at least a third less expense in every article. The difference of wood at five dollars and half a cord without cartage, of three dollars a load is very great. A neat delightful mansion at 200 dollars instead of 350, entirely new, in the French style of folding windows and recesses is also great. My boys are finally received in the college by the voluntary offering of these kind beings who are the professors without the least expense, which saves me Filicchi's 400 dollars—Mr. Robert Barry, the consul for Portugal, with his amiable wife, are unceasing in their kindness. They have taken care of my children for me during my journey and assisted me in every way. A very good servant at 4 ½ dollars per month does my washing, cleaning, and cooking. I have one pensioner only, but have two more engaged—several have offered as day scholars which does not enter in my plan, which I confine to 8 boarders for the first year or two. The best masters of music, drawing, etc., attend the seminary, which enables me to procure their services if necessary at a very reasonable rate.

The children are in a dream of delight on being once more united and so much caressed—but as it is all a novelty and consequently bears its best appearance, it is liable to change. However, I shall not be disappointed. While I make you this detail, my love, your mind may not be even in a situation to read it. Oh my Julia, [I wish] that I was this hour by your side—you will not deny me the one request—to write as soon as you can.

I had saved at interest five hundred dollars of your money; the bill you sent made six, and the four of Filicchi's for the last year (you are the only persons I receive from), made me the rich possessor of 1000 dollars when I arrived here. Therefore, do not be uneasy for us in that respect.

I shall write again, dearest, as soon as I hear from you—give my most affectionate remembrance to your dear amiable Maria—and particularly tell me of the health of our dear sister.

Always yours most truly

EASeton

ی‌هی‌هی‌هی‌ه

10th October [1808][127]

My own dear Julia,

I might challenge the whole world to produce a friend so sincere and constant as yourself; imagining that you would be quite impatient at my long silence, this very morning I determined that no impediment should prevent my asking you before night the question—if you thought any longer of your poor little nun, or if you did not expect to see her death announced in the paper—when behold the kindest, consoling letter from your dear self was unexpectedly handed to me. You are then really returned to home, and in safety, dear, dear Julia what would I not give to put my heart in your hands for a few hours. Since there is no hope of seeing you at least this autumn, let me answer your questions as nearly as possible—and in the first place tell you what will please you most. I would not change my situation for any possible advantage that could be offered to me under the sun—every endearing attention most congenial to human nature is bestowed upon us as freely as the air we breathe. My dear little dwelling is retirement and peace itself. I have but four boarders,[128] but those with my three girls are as many as I can manage this winter. In the spring if I get rid of a pleasant pain in the breast which has weakened me so much as to leave me little hope of the health in which you left me, then some proper assistance will be procured to enable me to extend my number. You know my disposition, dearest, sickness does not frighten the secret peace of mind which is founded on a confidence in

---

[127] 5.11, *Seton Collected Writings*, 2:37.

[128] The four boarders included: Aglaé Dubourg, Celanire Delarue, Isabella O'Conway of Philadelphia, and Julia Le Breton (Britton).

the Divine Goodness. If death succeeds it, I must put a Mother's hopes and fears in His Hands who has promised most to the widow and the fatherless.[129] Be assured there is no cause of serious apprehension for the present. The physician who attends the College is very eminent and knows perfectly the nature of such complaints as most French physicians do.[130] Instead of blisters, I take a bottle of Porter a day,[131] since which I am so strengthened and relieved that without doubt my complaint proceeded from weakness, especially as the cold bracing weather agrees with me so well. Although since one fortnight of hot weather in June, we have scarcely felt one day too warm.

Your Anna Maria is my great assistance and a finer creature both in mind and body you could scarcely wish for—since she is in Baltimore the woman is so marked in her appearance and manner that indeed, you would scarcely know her. Her chest is very prominent and the shoulders quite in their right place. Here she appears to advantage as the girls associated with her dress in some style and she of course imperceptibly adopts their manner.

October 10th.

My darling Julia, the above was written a week ago—the weather grew cold so suddenly that a general rout must be made for winter clothes and my letter was left to sleep in my Bible; again to return to your questions of kindness and love. My boys appear to be the most innocent and well disposed children that can be imagined for their age. Neither of them appear to me to show any distinct marks of genius, but their progress in their classes is superior to that of most boys of 10 and 12. William will be 12 in November, Anna Maria was 13 the third of last May—but your little Kate has more talents than either of the three elder, and Rebecca more than all of them together. The charm of being all reunited is still in full force. They are all happiness and love, though often they appear much affected if they see me suffer. Not one of them but anticipates the sorrow of being dispersed—but I myself have no fears on the subject—

---

[129] Cf. Psalm 146:9.

[130] Dr. Pierre Chatard of Baltimore was a physician who had studied in France before settling in Baltimore where he and his wife, Marie Françoise, became friends with the Setons and the Sisters of Charity. His granddaughter entered the Sisters of Charity August 28, 1857, and became Sister Julianna Chatard (1832-1917).

[131] Blisters were formed by the application of an irritating ointment or plaster as a medical treatment. Porter is a type of stout or ale.

How happy you are in your precious Maria! Oh what a Treasure is such a daughter. You do not tell me if Mr. John [Scott][132] is at Philadelphia or at Easton—nor a word of my dear Brother.[133] Poor Charlotte—how hard it must be to have no prospect of relief—I have always heard that complaint is without remedy, but I believe it does not speedily destroy the constitution.

You talk of being old! Believe me until you told me our dear Maria is near 21, I never recollected that you are older than myself, and as I am full 35, I wish you joy—now pray tell me, Julia, if it is possible that with your intelligent mind, long experience of human vicissitudes and very critical moment of life, tell me if you do not sometimes reflect on the long, long, long, long life to come? If you do, and in earnest, your own friend has one of the first wishes and prayers of her heart answered. Answer me this question in some moment that you are alone with God. I will never preach to you, but I wish I could pour my heart in your bosom and tell you how sweet it is to have Him our Best Friend, [our] Dearest Hope. Do, do promise that you will pray to Him for this knowledge. You are sure of being heard with peculiar pleasure. He would leave his ninety-nine[134] in a moment, if you would but be in earnest in begging His assistance. You and I must die, dear, daily—Oh, do do think of it. Poor Maria how much better an inheritance you might leave her than riches.

Your suggestion that you may possibly come to Baltimore[135] is most sweet. How I should delight in putting my darlings again in your arms and once more be in them myself. I hope by the spring you will find our prospects better. [Antonio] Filicchi writes me he has been on an embassy for the Queen of Naples, and that some fortunate speculation has doubled his fortune. He gives me unlimited credit on *Murray & Sons*[136] but I have written him explicitly and suggested my wish to do something advantageous with the lot of ground these kind Gentlemen of the Seminary and College have given us.

---

[132] Julia's son, John Morin Scott.

[133] Samuel Sitgreaves, a brother of Julia Sitgreaves Scott, was a lawyer in Easton, Pennsylvania. He also served as a member of the Pennsylvania House of Representatives and later as a representative of the United States government in England.

[134] Cf. Matthew 18:12.

[135] Julia Scott never came to Baltimore to visit Elizabeth.

[136] The Filicchi business agent in the United States.

You ask my terms. They are 200 dollars per year—extra accomplishments which require the assistance of Masters, such as music, dancing, drawing, etc., are paid separately. The Masters engaged in the service of the College attend at my house on the most moderate terms though they are the best that can be procured. Everybody here seems to pity the poor little widow.

You could hardly believe my baker's bill from the college. For three full months is 8 dollars 88/100, the butcher's 18 dollars 50/100, and the best wood including cartage 4 dollars 25/100 a cord—very different from New York where I have often paid 3 dollars 25/100 per load in winter, but this is owing to the College stipulation.

You are too good, my Julia. You cannot think how I am delighted that you propose sending your clothing now out of use. Do not send the best, nor fear that anything can be useless. All turns to account with me, particularly anything of John's for my boys. Their clothes are my heaviest expense—and all my trunks now are nearly empty. You know I never had much—your gown Anna Maria wore without any alteration but the slope behind. My direction[137] is to the care of Reverend Mr. Dubourg, St Mary's College, Baltimore. Write me when you send them, and I shall get them safe.

dear friend Yours ever EAS

6th December 1808[138]

Oh my own dear Julia,

How long a time you must have been uneasy for your poor friend. The sight of the dear amiable John Cox[139] brought the whole recollection with full force, and convinced me the hours and days pass with me much faster than I calculate. From half past five in the morning until 9 at night every moment is full, no space even to be troubled. Ten girls, three of them almost women, keep the wheel going continually. Many very advantageous offers of assistants have presented themselves, but in the present state of my

---

[137] Elizabeth's address in Baltimore.

[138] 5.13, *Seton Collected Writings,* 2:41.

[139] Julia's nephew, John Cox, of Philadelphia, was a son of James and Charlotte Sitgreaves Cox.

family, we are so happy and live so much as a Mother surrounded by her children that I cannot resolve to admit a stranger, yet it must be eventually. What would amuse you, my darling friend, would be to see your old lady at five in the afternoon (as soon as school is over), seated gravely with a slate and pencil with a Master of Arithmetic, stuffing her brain with dollars, cents, and fractions, and actually going over the studies, both in grammar and figures, which are suited to the scholar better than the mistress. So it is. You may well imagine there is very little time for writing. Even at this moment the pen is falling from my hand so completely is nature wearied.

8th December 1808—

John Cox gives me a most interesting account of you all. How it delights me that Charlotte [Sitgreaves Cox] is so much recovered, and he says you have perfect health. Yet the idea of that certain will is very painful, and as it relates to our dear amiable Maria, it is more than painful—precious, precious child—her reward is ever with her. I think the person to whom the property has fallen is in a most embarrassing situation—for me every dollar would be a thorn. Why do I speak of this to you—but can I love and honor Maria's conduct so much without being sensible of her disappointment in being denied the testimony so much her due.

And so, my darling friend, you are still the woman of fashion—still drawing the chains of the World—alas—my soul sighs—that subject will not do.

It would be a great pleasure to you to see my girls. Anna Maria's spirits are so even and independent that you would hardly believe she was in a transport at the sight of the white beaver hat especially as Miss [Aglaé] Dubourg has one exactly like it. They are two lovely beings and very much united. Rebecca wears the brown one, and Kitty had a brown one also, presented to her accidentally. Everybody is pleased, and Mother enjoys it as much as they do. Dear, dear Julia, many things you have sent were of too much value for such children, but care will not be wanting. They are much more useful to us than you would perhaps imagine, as I am obliged to be more attentive to appearance here than in New York—not myself, but the family. Poor little self is always dressed for the grave which must ever be my dearest anticipation tho' not in the sense you take it darling.

How truly was I mortified to find our Maria gone, and without one word to you or a single call from me who would have walked five miles to have seen her again, but so it was, that it was out of the question as to the possibility of going to her, even if I had not had the mistaken idea that Mrs. Harper[140] lived at a distance from the city, which afterwards our Bishop [John] Carroll informed me is not the case. I have confounded the idea of Mrs. Caton's[141] residence with hers.

I am obliged so strictly to avoid giving offence that as I could not leave home at any time without the greatest inconvenience, I do not pretend to leave it at all. This, as you know, is one of the charms of my situation, which truly and indeed, my Julia, is most congenial to all my ideas of happiness. Oh how sweet to be every moment employed in the service and in the sight of the dearest and most generous of Masters who repays with the tenderness of compassionate love even the good will of his child, however imperfect its execution. But you do not understand—poor Julia.

Will you please, dearest, send my warmest, tenderest [regards] to Brother Sam [Sitgreaves], and tell your dear Charlotte my heart was light as a feather at the sight of her amiable son who [is worthy] of her, and had it not been for the fear of surprising him, I should have given him such a squeeze as I wish to give to her.

Oh my dear, dear Julia, when I think of you all and of you, my first, last, and most faithful friend—my friend who has borne so many years with all my negligence, and who is unchangeable through so many changes. I would wish to lay at your feet, to be your servant, anything that might be the least expression of my attachment to you and yours, but such is the Divine Order that the good must be received on my part, and not bestowed. I must be content with that dispensation which heightens his favors by conveying them through a hand so dear and beloved.

I am now so well, so free from weakness of the breast, etc., that I can hardly believe it. Winter has always been my cheerful season, and here I am sheltered from all cold and changes of weather, wet walks, etc.

Dear, dear friend, farewell.

Your EAS

---

[140] Catherine Carroll, a daughter of Charles and Mary Darnell Carroll of Carrollton, married major-General Robert Goodloe Harper. They had three daughters, Elizabeth, Mary Diana, and Emily, who were cousins of John Carroll, archbishop of Baltimore.

[141] Mary (Polly) Carroll, a daughter of Charles and Mary Darnell Carroll of Carrollton, married Richard Caton. They had four daughters, Louisa, Mary Ann, Elizabeth, and Emily, who were cousins of John Carroll, archbishop of Baltimore.

Give my dear Maria my love and blessing, and thank my dear John Scott for the cloth.

My darling Julia, John Cox is detained here so long that I shall have time to write again by him and conclude to send this little word of love by a person who leaves [with] this for Philadelphia tomorrow

May a thousand, thousand blessings, and the first and best of blessings be yours the ensuing years—even to Eternal ages, my dear, dear friend.

December 18th.

2nd March 1809[142]

My own darling Julia,

I think my last letter must have given you painful impressions respecting the poor little Mother's heart which was, to be sure at that time rather depressed and with some reason, but gradually its pain has worn away as nothing new has occurred to increase the weight. I think our beloved Anna will not be materially injured by the strong necessity which has forced her to exertions I really had thought her incapable of—it seems as if the moment she was made sensible of the uneasiness and sorrow she occasioned me, the terror and alarm of her mind banished every fancy and imagination which has blinded her. She became docile and attentive to <u>my will</u> as if it was not opposed to her own. Poor dear child, I do not know how she can be so patient, as I well remember at her age I should not have been, neither seeing nor hearing from the dearly beloved.

Emily Caton is not quite so generous.[143] Her family is truly unhappy about her, but what can be expected from a warm heart and lively imagination nourished only by romances—poor, poor child.

As you have so long shared all my pains, my dearest, how much pleasure it will give you to know that Providence has disposed for me a plan after my own heart—a Benevolent gentleman[144] of this place has formed a

---

[142] 5.20, *Seton Collected Writings*, 1:58.

[143] Emily Caton McTavish was a daughter of Richard and Mary Carroll Caton, both of well-known Maryland families. She married John McTavish in 1816, remained in Maryland, and managed her grandfather Charles Carroll's households.

[144] Samuel Sutherland Cooper.

scheme of establishing a manufactory for the use of the poor, and includes in his intention the education of children, rich and poor.[145] He is about purchasing a place at Emmitsburg,[146] some distance from Baltimore, not very considerable, and has offered me the department of taking care of the children who may be presented, or rather of being the Mother of the family. This pleases me for many reasons—in the first place, I shall live in the mountains; in the next, I shall see no more of the world than if I was out of it, and have every object centered in my own family, both of provision [and] employment, etc.

A very amiable young lady, who has been my assistant[147] two months past, will accompany me, and with Miss Nicholson [whom] I before mentioned to you and Mr. [William] Dubourg's niece, compose an invaluable society for Annina.[148] Such is the prospect, dearest, but whether it is to be accomplished or not is the question. I am quite at my ease on the subject, caring very little how I am disposed of the remainder of my life, if only I may persevere in acting the Mother's part with fidelity. The care of teaching will be off my hands tho' not the superintendence. I do not hesitate to embrace the offer of going to the country, as no doubt it will be a means of prolonging my days for my dear ones, and probably be an effectual means of extricating Anna Maria from the effects of her imprudence. For if young DuPavillon is hereafter true to his attachment, he may easily claim her; if not, her happiness depends on seeing him no more.

Are you not happy, most happy in your Maria [Scott]—but she never had the milk of an inflammable Mother as poor Anna Maria had.

---

[145] Elizabeth established Saint Joseph's Free School February 22, 1810, and Saint Joseph's Academy May 14, 1810. Families from throughout the United States enrolled their daughters.

[146] The town of Emmitsburg in the Catoctin spur of the Blue Ridge Mountains traces its roots to Charles Carroll of Annapolis who sold 2260 acres in 1757 to Samuel Emmit who deeded his son William 35 acres upon which the lots of a new town called Emmitsburg were laid out in 1785. The town was incorporated in 1825. Located 52 miles west of Baltimore, it was an early center of Catholicism in western Maryland.

[147] Sister Cecilia O'Conway of Philadelphia, who was the first American Sister of Charity.

[148] Rebecca (Becky) Nicholson and Aglaé Dubourg were both students in Elizabeth's school. Rebecca Nicholson was the daughter of Joseph Hooper Nicholson of Baltimore, the brother-in-law of Francis Scott Key and the one who first arranged for the printing of the poem "Defence of Fort M'Henry" which was set to the tune of "Anacreon in Heaven" and became known as "The Star-Spangled Banner."

My Julia, when you write me, say if you have disposed of the funds which the embargo had embarrassed you with as our John Scott informed me, and if you would choose to lend three thousand or two thousand dollars on the best security in either Philadelphia or Baltimore, to be refunded in a year. This question you will [please] answer as to a stranger. Perhaps you will think it very strange. I ask it but as I only do it in fulfillment of a promise—answer it and then forget it. How you laugh at me, but did you never make a promise in a hurry. Yet, if indeed you have anything to dispose of in that way, you may command the security [of] Mr. Sims, or James Craig, or receive a mortgage on the best lots of ground in Philadelphia. It will be employed in the purchase of, or rather the arrangement of my future dwelling, to be sure, but you are not to consider me in the case.

As I have been already three days writing this letter at intervals, if it is not concluded it may be another week. So, again and again, the repetition of a thousand times, ten thousand blessings on you, dearest, with my tenderest love to your dear children. Do not forget to tell me how dear Charlotte is. This lovely weather I hope will strengthen her. Is Brother Sam well? Is his sum of multiplication enlarged? Tell me all about yourself and yours.

Your own friend *EAS*

ৡৡৡৡৡৡ

23rd March 1809[149]

My own dear Julia, kindest and dearest of friends—

Your letter speaks a language to me which requires the most unreserved explanation of the circumstances which interest you.[150] This is the history of them, a Mr. [Samuel] Cooper, an Englishman of fortune and great talents from a singular combination of circumstances has attached himself to the Catholic Church. I met him on my first arrival here and travelled with

---

[149] 5.21, *Seton Collected Writings*, 2:61.
[150] In her letter of March 15, Julia raised several objections to Elizabeth's proposed plan of moving from Baltimore.

him to George Town.[151] He had then made the resolution of taking Holy Orders, and as you know, I had long since renounced everything like earthly attachments. From the involuntary attraction of certain dispositions to each other, there was, however, an interest and esteem understood. You may be sure, tho' I have always considered him as a consecrated being as he did me, and the only result of this partiality has been the encouragement of each other to persevere in the path which each had chosen. In consequence of his having now taken the Tonsure, he has given his reasons to his brother[152] for disposing of his own property, and has purchased a very valuable farm[153] forty miles from this place, on which all the conveniences of life are abundant. This farm and its appurtenances are placed in the hands of Mr. [William] Dubourg[154] for your own friend's accommodation and future home, as a sure living and maintenance. The views of Mr. Cooper always have been to afford instruction and consolation to the poor, in every way it can be applied to them. He proposes to have a manufactory on this farm, it is true, but neither the fatigue nor responsibility will fall on me, you may rest assured. It is true, also, that I shall be at the head of a community which will live under the strictest rules of order and regularity, but I shall not give those laws, nor have any care of compelling others to fulfill them. If any person embraces them and afterwards chooses to infringe them, they will only find in me a friend to admonish and it will be in the hands of Mr. Dubourg, either to rectify or dismiss them. The order of Sulpicians, which is composed by

---

[151] Shortly after her arrival in Baltimore in 1808, Elizabeth, accompanied by Rev. Michael Hurley, O.S.A., and Mr. Samuel Sutherland Cooper, had traveled to Georgetown College where her sons had been studying near Washington. She brought them back with her and enrolled them in Saint Mary's College in Baltimore.

[152] This may be either his brother James Cooper or his half-brother Commodore Richard Dale. In 1813 Elizabeth wrote Julia Scott about an attempt by Cooper's brother to recoup the donation Samuel Cooper had made to the Sisters of Charity.

[153] Samuel Cooper paid $6,961 for the Fleming Farm which included two tracts of 212 acres and 57 acres. The deed was recorded April 26, 1809, in the name of Samuel Cooper and William Dubourg of Baltimore county and John Dubois of Frederick, County, Maryland.

[154] At the time the farm was purchased for the Sisters of Charity, the community had not yet been incorporated and Rev. Louis Dubourg, S.S., was the superior. When he left Maryland in 1815, Dubourg relinquished his legal rights to the property to Samuel Cooper and Rev. John Duobis, S.S. The community was incorporated in 1817 and two years later Cooper and Dubois transferred their rights and the titles of the property to the Sisters of Charity of St. Joseph's, Inc.

the venerable and respectable gentlemen of this Seminary and College,[155] have a Seminary and a great part of their property at Emmitsburg on the Mountains[156] where the farm in question is situated. The most ancient of them always presides and resides there. I shall be always protected and taken care of as a part of their family. I cannot help wishing extremely that I may be so fortunate, as to merit a continuance of their friendship.

So far [as] I can express, but to speak the joy of my soul at the prospect of being able to assist the poor, visit the sick, comfort the sorrowful, clothe little innocents, and teach them to love God! There I must stop. The present living I have, if it would continue, is enough to content me, but out of seven girls, I have had in my charge, four are withdraw[n], not from any discontent with me, but because they (two of them are older than Anna) have accomplished the allotted time when their year is out, which will be in June—the time proposed for my departure, nor do any parents show a disposition to commit their children to your friend on any other pretence than that of rectifying their tempers and giving them good sentiments. I will venture to say that even yourself, Sister Charlotte, or any other, however attached to me, would not give me the charge of children you meant to bring up for the world, or to bear a part in polished society. If you could conceive the wretched state of my health in summer, and know what I suffered during the last, you would be quite reconciled that I should breathe the mountain air at least for a while. If I live a year or two, as Mr. Cooper intends to form here a boarding school for girls of family, I shall either be at the head of it with such persons as now carry on those establishments here, or at least be able to put my Kitty and Rebecca in an advantageous situation. Anna Maria in her present state will be very well in the country for the summer, if she has the least wish to be [away] from it, I shall give her over to you. You would never, never say no to a friend, in such a case.

The love you have ever shown me excites in me an unbounded confidence, my darling friend, but I entreat you that this letter may be as secret as the grave, in all that relates to Mr. Cooper. I think you must have met with him as he was a frequent visitor at Mrs. Craig's, and an intimate friend of Mrs. Patterson.

---

[155] The Sulpicians operated Saint Mary's Seminary and Saint Mary's College, Baltimore.

[156] Mount St. Mary's College near Emmitsburg, Maryland, was founded in 1808 by Rev. John Dubois, S.S., as a school for boys. It became a seminary as well. It was located at the base of Saint Mary's Mountain on land donated by a prominent local Catholic family, the Elders.

How little room I have to speak to you of your dear self, and particularly to ask you why, when you have so many calls for money, you continually send me so much where it can so easily be dispensed with. Do not do it again, dearest, unless I ask you, which I sacredly promise to do if there is the least necessity. The necessary cash for the payment of the farm was immediately obtained from the brother of Mr. Cooper who was very glad to pay him the full value of his Philadelphia lots, as property of that kind is now so valuable. I will very soon write you again my Julia—say to me whatever you will—you can never in anything do otherwise than give me redoubled proofs of your interest and affection for us. I hope when you consider the temper, habits, and disposition of your own friend. You will not absolutely disapprove of her resolution which leaves her as much, and even more liberty, than she now enjoys. Love and cherish in your heart the one who loves you as her own soul.

ever your *EAS*

৵৵৵৵৵৵

9th May 1809[157]

My dearest dear Julia,

To see Brother once more, and to know that you are all well, what a pleasure for your friend—I need not dwell on the feelings—the remembrances—the sight of him revived—you may conceive them. When he turned from my door, I felt a melancholy and aching at my heart which I thought it now incapable of—having suppressed every expression of sentiment in his presence as he was accompanied by Mr. [William] Dubourg who awes me extremely. When he was gone, I felt that nature would accompany me to the grave although, indeed my Julia, I do try to take everything just as it comes and to be independent of every external object except my children and my friend. For you may rely upon it, that while one spark of life remains, I shall love you with unremitting tenderness, though [Divine] Providence has so ordered it that it is never in my power to prove it to you.

The middle of next month, as my house is then to be given up, we intend to leave Baltimore. You would hardly believe a creature, once so ardent in every wish could be so indifferent about the place of residence

---

[157] 5.26, *Seton Collected Writings*, 2:68.

or the circumstances which are to attend it, except that the state of bodily weakness which sometimes threatens my dear ones with the loss of Mother's care, makes me desire rather to go to the country air, as it hitherto has been my infallible remedy for every complaint.

But, oh the Blessed Will of Him who rules both life and death be done. Now, my dear friend, in His Name I entreat you to be perfectly at ease on my account—every comfort and indulgence I could even wish for will be mine. Mr. Dubourg has appointed a very amiable lady,[158] who perfectly understands the management of things, [as] steward of the family. She is much younger and more active than myself, and of course I must at stated times inspect her accounts. Having almost as many assistants as there are now children going with us; and having an ample supply of all the good things [which] a substantial country farm can produce—poultry, milk, etc., etc.—you can have no reason to be in the least anxious for us. If you could imagine how kind and attentive a Father we find in Mr. Dubourg, you would not have a moments care on the subject. The Superior[159] of our Seminary here who is graced with all the venerable qualities of seventy-five which is his age—a mind still strong and alive to the interest of our little family, as if we were all his own, and one of the most elegant men in his manners you ever met with, is going to take the charge of our community and reside at Emmitsburg, which is a great consolation to me in every sense. He will say Mass for us every day, regulate our religious exercises, etc. In short, dearest, while you will be solicitous for me in your visionary scenes, I shall be enjoying substantial and solid peace which you know is all we should ever wish for.

I must hasten this hasty scribble to Brother, as he says he positively goes tomorrow. A thousand, thousand, thousand blessings be with you, my own Julia. Love your own friend always. My tender love to Maria and dear John. Tell him I don't thank him for oversleeping himself the morning Brother left Philadelphia.

MEASeton

---

[158] Anastasia Nabbs.
[159] Rev. Charles Nagot, S.S. As a result of an accident and ill health, Nagot never went to Emmitsburg as superior of the Sisters of Charity.

20th September 1809[160]

Oh my Julia,

What a letter have I received from you. Who but yourself could have written it to your friend who seemed to have forgotten you. About a month ago I wrote you in a very lively mood—a parcel of nonsense about your abandoning me, imagining I wore a straight waistcoat and giving you some droll idea of my position—which letter would illy reply to your dear,[161] tender expression—therefore, seriously and sincerely, I will answer all your questions one by one. In the first place, never was I more at liberty or in a happier state of mind to answer and make every communication to the dear ones of my heart of whom you ever must be the first. Why I have not written, or rather sent what I wrote, is only another proof of that careless disposition so often lamented; and also from a certainty that you were not at home and probably would not be until the fall. As to affection, Julia, and the tenderest solicitude for all that concerned you—the tears gush at the thought you could have reason to doubt it—yet you know not that the nearer a soul is truly united to God the more its sensibilities are increased to every being of his creation much more to those whom it is bound to love by the tenderest and most endearing ties.

You will hear a thousand reports of nonsense about our community, which I beg you not to mind. The truth is we have the best ingredients of happiness—order, peace, and solitude. There are only 16 now in [the] family—a steward who supplies all our outdoor wants—a housekeeper who regulates within [Kitty Mullan], a superintendent of the work room, and my

[160] 6.7, *Seton Collected Writings,* 2:82.

[161] Elizabeth Seton's usage of "would illy reply" probably means that her response to Julia would be inadequate.

dear Cecilia[162] (who takes charge of my children and two dear little girls[163] I brought from Baltimore)—take all fatigue and care off my hands as much as if I was a child myself. I am a name to keep up regularity and to say there is a head to the house. The chief work I do is to walk about with my knitting in my hand (we supply, or, are to supply, knitting and spinning [for] the college and two seminaries[164] of Mr. [William] Dubourg with socks and cloth). [I] give my opinion, see that everyone is in their place, write letters, read, and give good advice.

Your Anna makes you uneasy, but again I assure you circumstanced as she is with young DuPavillon, she is a thousand times happier here than she could be elsewhere. She has no restraint or want of amusement—nothing can be more pleasant than our situation as to woods, meadows, etc., the comforts of life in plenty. Cecilia and Harriet are the companions of her choice, if she had a thousand. She studies French, Spanish, and Italian with them under a Mistress who is sweetness and modesty itself, a Miss [Cecilia O'] Conway, daughter of the Spanish teacher in Philadelphia. Her progress will never be of any consequence, probably, but she is pleased and it keeps her busy. Indeed, my Julia, if you had her, she would be a source of perpetual uneasiness to you for, as she grows up and looses herself from that blind obedience exacted from a child under thirteen, she takes many varieties of temper which makes her disposition so unequal, that until she is more mature and experience teaches her some necessary lessons, it is very difficult to make her happy. The great error now past, and irreparable on my part, is to have made her my friend and companion, too soon; few dispositions

---

[162] Cecilia O'Conway (1788-1865) from Philadelphia became the first member of the American Sisters of Charity when she joined Elizabeth in Baltimore December 7, 1808. Known as Sister Cecilia (Vero or Cis), she was elected to the first council in 1809. She made the first novitiate in Emmitsburg (1812-1813) and pronounced vows July 19, 1813. A teacher at Saint Joseph's Academy, she was elected treasurer of the community (1816 and 1817), but in her second term, in order to relieve some problems with carrying out the treasurer's responsibilities, Elizabeth agreed to keep the books and assist her. Soon she was missioned to New York (1817) to work with the orphans, but she returned to Saint Joseph's (1819) temporarily because of poor health. In 1823 Cecilia transferred to the cloistered Ursuline community in Quebec City where she was known as Mother Marie of the Incarnation. She retained happy memories and a correspondence with her Emmitsburg friends until her death.

[163] Isabella O'Conway and Julia LeBreton who had been students of Mrs. Seton at her school on Paca Street.

[164] Saint Mary's Seminary in Baltimore and Mount St. Mary's Seminary in Emmitsburg.

like your dear amiable Maria can bear to be advanced so soon, but all will be right at last with the excellent examples she has in both her aunts.

Cecilia's complaint of the breast[165] so far remains, that it is impossible for her to undertake the burden of cares she left at home in the charge of housekeeper and teacher in James Seton's family.[166] Besides that, some delicate circumstances of a connection he has formed make it extremely improper any young female should reside there. Here she finds a house after her own heart, and the summit of all earthly desires which is to live with me.

Barclay[167] has written poor Harriet a proposal that he should remain eight or ten years longer in Jamaica to obtain a fortune. She is so shocked with a proposal, which so evidently shows his indifference to her, that it seems to disgust her with everything of the kind. However, I hope he will know how to appreciate her merit and constancy and things may be accommodated in a shorter time. She has resolved to wait the event patiently, and make the best use of her time in the interval. Anna and Cecilia are the gainers and she is determined to hide her disappointment in our Mountains and keep out of the circles of fashion this winter, which would be impossible if she returned to New York.

I wish Sister Charlotte's curiosity southward had been awakened before we left Baltimore. I think you will all come to see me next summer and take a laugh at our black gowns and demure looks, which, however, hide a set of as lively merry hearts as ever met together. My darling sweet boys are here, also all health and life. They came just in the vacation and I found they would be so well in the Seminary here, which has equal advantage with the one in Baltimore without such a multitude of boys that I obtained from Mr. [William] Dubourg a place. Every Wednesday they are in Mother's arms. It is such a comfort to have all within my reach you well know. The note you enclosed my darling friend was very, very unexpected—the House of Murrey in New York informed me through Brother [Samuel] Craig that they have no more funds of the Filicchis, which I cannot understand—nor have I heard from Leghorn since I left New York except by a brother-in-

---

[165] Elizabeth's youngest sister-in-law, Cecilia Seton had tuberculosis.

[166] Cecilia Seton had been living in the home of her brother James and caring for his eight motherless children before her arrival in Baltimore.

[167] Andrew Barclay Bayley, Elizabeth's half-brother who was engaged to Harriet Seton, had gone to Jamaica by 1806 in order to pursue a mercantile career.

law of the Filicchi's, who tells me they made a hundred thousand dollars during the Embargo by some fortunate speculation while everyone here was losing. Their constant friendship I cannot doubt, so that I hope soon for some explanation. Your love in the meantime supplies all. We should not have suffered for anything however a more generous set of beings than those whose hands I am in you cannot imagine. Never have the least apprehension on that score—if you knew half the really good your friend possesses while the world thinks she is deprived of everything worth having, you would moralize an hour at least and allow that she has truly and really the best of it. If I am not strong in health, it is because my constitution is broken; air, exercise, good food, indolence, and content ought to strengthen me, but so long a combat as I have gone through will leave its vestiges. Yet there is no settled complaint of any kind—one strong northwester will brace all again—how I wish you could take it with me.

What are you doing darling, dear Glorianna?[168] You are well, you have many comforts, but you have not all. When you are taken to the sick bed, what will you say You will acknowledge [that] you have had enough—too much of this world because it has bound you—but you will feel a want which nothing then can supply. The long, long, long life in perspective will seem a strange land with strange inhabitants—think about it a little—do you know, dearest, that after all my neglect of you and the little reason you have to think I love you with the boundless tenderness, I do love you with—God is My Witness, I would this moment gladly give my life to obtain for you the comforts to be obtained in that hour—the Peace of a Soul going to its kindest dearest tenderest Friend. Hush! You understand! When I think of you sometimes, I could go and tear you away from all and wrap you in the bosom that loves and has loved you so long. What would I not do to give you only a little taste—dear, dear, dear friend. You laugh—but while you laugh consider [the following]—

What an extravagant idea it is that piety creates gloominess and disgust. Unacquainted with the anticipations of a soul whose views are chiefly pointed to another existence, it is inconceivable what liberty it enjoys—the cares and troubles of life surround it, to be sure as others, but how different their effect—human passions and weakness, to be sure, are never extinct but they cannot triumph in the heart which is possessed by this Friend of Love and Peace. She is very lovely, Julia—make acquaintance with her—she will

[168] An affectionate name for Julia Scott.

not be angry [that] you have neglected her so long. Do you want a letter of recommendation? She will receive you even without that. Tell me in your next [letter] how you like her—and if Maria has any sentiment in her favor. A thousand, thousand, thousand blessings be with you, dearest. To the last moment of my life I will love you, pray for you, and long for your happiness—it shall not be so long before you hear from me again.

forever ever your own friend *EAS*

Direct to me as usual[169]

27th December 1809[170]

My own dear little Julia,

How do you do? Are your dear ones well? I have had many heavy hours since I wrote you—first from the extreme illness of Cecilia [Seton] which terminated in an abscess of the liver, and now the death of my sweet and darling Harriet, who was the life and joy of my heart for many months past.[171] Her illness has been long; that is, since she first complained of the sick head ache and bilious affliction, she has been long subject to, but sometimes better, at others worse, I had not the least alarm till her complaint took a sudden turn. Nature took a wrong course and she lost so much—excessive debility succeeded, her head became violently affected, and the dear child could neither be helped by blisters nor any etceteras of medical aid.

So it goes with your friend, tribulation is my element. If it only carries me home [to Eternity] at last, never mind the present, do you ever think about it, my dearest, dearest Julia? Year after year passes, the last must come—foolish and extravagant as your own friend now appears to you, when the scene is about to close, things will wear so different an appearance, you would be very glad to have been among the number of those who look beyond it. Is it not so dearest?

Our Mountains[172] are very black but the scene below bright and gay—the meadows still green and my dear ones skipping upon them with the sheep, except poor Anna Maria who deeply feels the loss of her companion

[169] Elizabeth Seton reminds her friend to use the same address.
[170] 6.14, *Seton Collected Writings,* 2:94
[171] Harriet Seton died December 23, 1809.
[172] The Catoctin spur of the Blue Ridge Mountains.

friend and adviser.[173] They always walked together, read and worked together, sharing even the same bed. Yet, I am much reconciled to our loss as her situation with [Andrew] Barclay [Bayley] was so distressing—always fearing he was only bound to her by honor, or if his affection continued, was obliged to follow him to Jamaica or probably to give him up entirely. She was an angelic girl, truly, and her death is one of the hard blows destined for your own friend. Yet, here I go like iron or rock, day after day—as He pleases, and how He pleases, but, to be sure, when my turn comes, I shall be very glad. Say, dearest, say if you are growing good, and how everything goes with you and our dear Maria and John. Is Mrs. [Charlotte Sitgreaves] Cox able to bear the change of weather? Is our dear, dear Brother Sam still at Easton? Is he well? If it was in my power to bring on you all the many blessings I wish you—you would have thousands more than you can even wish for yourselves.

I do not like to send this blank side [of paper] but have several letters to write by this post, dearest. They tell me a hundred most ridiculous stories[174] are going about relative to our manner of living here, but I hope you will not listen to them a moment, if they should reach you. Believe me again when I assure you that I have, with my darlings, also true peace and comfort [in] every way. As to sickness, and death itself, if it comes to us again, we know that they are the common attendants of human life. They are our certain portion at one period or other, and it would be madness to be unhappy because I am treated like the rest of human beings. So do not give it a thought for my share in them, but think, dearest, think for your own precious most precious self, my Gloriana farewell—

ever your own friend *EASeton*

---

[173] Harriet Seton.

[174] Gouverneur and Charlotte Seton Ogden, Elizabeth's brother-in-law and sister-in-law, wrote several letters to Harriet Seton berating her for remaining in Maryland and converting to Catholicism. Vehemently anti-Catholic in their sentiments, they had been critical of Elizabeth while she was still in New York.

Conclusion

Elizabeth Seton wrote the preceding correspondence on themes of family, faith, and friendship to persons closest to her at the time of William Magee's fatal illness, her conversion, and subsequent struggle to provide for her children as a widow. These letters offer glimpses into her heart and soul. Their lines offer enlightenment on the paths that led into soul-searching and life-changing decisions that transformed Elizabeth into a saint who continues to inspire others through her example.

Circumstances and events, both in New York and Livorno, provided the context in which Elizabeth opted for radical change and a new way of life. She found herself confronted with needs which she embraced as opportunities and challenges. Faced with harsh economic realities and limited options, she entered into faith-filled discernment about God's call, her religious persuasion, and her parental obligations to five fatherless children. These became the threads of life with which Elizabeth wove a new lifestyle of creative charity for herself and others. Elizabeth assumed new roles and responsibilities as a convert to Catholicism, foundress of a community, religious formator, and mentor.

The following excerpts from letters to three additional women provide further illustration of how Elizabeth's correspondence continued to weave her core values of family, faith, and friendship into a rich tapestry of sanctity and spirituality. These remain her lasting legacy for the Church and world of today.

Call to Religious Conversion

Having heard an inner call, Elizabeth spent time in study, prayer, and reflection prior to her decision to become a Roman Catholic. She shared her experience of discernment and conversion in the following draft written for a woman in Philadelphia, probably a relative of Mary Raborg, a pupil at Saint Joseph's Academy. In this letter Elizabeth explains to Mrs. William Raborg the circumstances which led to her conversion twelve years previously, providing spiritual insights about the consolation she has experienced since 1805.[1]

> I assure you my becoming a Catholic was a very simple
> consequence of going to [Italy], a Catholic country, where
> it was impossible for anyone interested in any religion, not

---

[1] 7.98, Elizabeth Seton to Mrs. William Raborg, [June 1817] *Seton Collected Writings*, 2:488.

to see the wide difference between the first established Faith given and founded by Our Lord and his apostles, and the various forms it has since taken. As I had always delighted in reading the Scriptures, I had so deep an impression of the mysteries of Divine Revelation, that though full of the sweet thought that every good and well meaning Soul was right, I determined when I came home [to New York], both in duty to my children and my own Soul, to learn all I was capable of understanding on the subject—if ever a Soul did make a fair inquiry, our God knows that mine did. Every day of life more and more increases my gratitude to Him for having made me what I am.

Certainly, though it was the knowledge of the Protestant doctrine with regard to Faith, which made me a Catholic— for as soon as on inquiry, I found that Episcopalians did not think everybody right, I was convinced my safe plan was to unite with the Church in which, at all events, they admitted that I would find salvation, and where also I would be secure of the Apostolic Succession, as well as of the many consolations which no other religion but the Catholic can afford. The whole is that with the convictions of my Conscience, my Salvation depended on embracing the Catholic Faith—I never obtrude my thoughts on the subject [with others] but leave all to their own light and grace, while I enjoy mine—a true joy to me indeed the daily morning Sacrifice [of the Mass] and our frequent, and daily [Holy] Communion, when prepared—what a contrast to the morning sleep in former days. It has been my wealth in poverty, and joy in deepest afflictions...

EASeton

Call to Live in Community for Mission of Service

Catherine Dupleix, better known as Dué, belonged to the inner circle which supported Elizabeth throughout her life regardless of life's ever changing circumstances. After Elizabeth was settled at Emmitsburg, she gathered the threads of recent events in order to bring Dué up to date about the Setons. She even refers to herself as a "shipwrecked friend"—probably meaning that the family prosperity had fallen into ruin. Dué's husband George Dupleix had been a regular correspondent with Elizabeth since Dué apparently wasn't inclined to letter writing.

In this letter Elizabeth gives an account of herself: her call to serve in community as a Sister of Charity. Elizabeth describes her vision of the community's mission as "schooling children, nursing the sick, and manufacturing for ourselves and the poor, which to my disposition you know is the sum of all earthly happiness."[2] At the time the following letter was written, Elizabeth had been living in Saint Joseph's Valley for one year. She also brings Dué up to date about her children, their hopes and dreams, as well as her concerns for them.[3]

> My own dear Dué!
>
> Never let it enter your thoughts that time, absence, or above all your carelessness in writing, can change, even in degree a love, a friendship of my soul which for so many years has been as a part of itself...your poor little shipwrecked friend is finishing her career under the strange and ill placed title of Abbess of a convent; I say ill placed because it is as much so as it would be to call me by any other name than that of Seton as the little community I have the charge of are bound by no obligations and are united only with the view of schooling children, nursing the sick, and manufacturing for ourselves and the poor, which to my disposition you know is the sum of all earthly happiness.
>
> It is hard to live so far from the first ties of my life, but you know circumstances sometimes made a residence among them rather painful than other ways at least it could not counter balance the comfort of having my darling children all around me, in a fine country where we enjoy the plain but substantial comforts of that kind of life which looks only to Home [Divine Providence] for its conveniences. We have a new and handsome house newly built on a very large farm half covered with woods. High mountains run all one side of it and meadows below. The darling Boys [sons William and

[2] 6.45, Elizabeth Seton to Catherine Dupleix, 4 June 1810, *Seton Collected Writings*, 2:136.
[3] Ibid.

Richard] are in a branch of the Baltimore college [Mount St. Mary's] half-way up the mountain and well taken care of [in] every way. Without partiality, they are two as sweet fellows in looks, manners and disposition as poor Mother's heart could wish. Richard always Mother's boy, all his desire centers in a farm that he may never quit her—William is the boy of hopes and fears. Reading some lines in an almanac the other day of the whistling of a sea boy in the main top shrouds—"that's your sorts" he said "I'm your man" and always talks of saving the World—but yet has great ideas of being a gentleman in everything, without knowing that a gentleman without a penny is but a name; however as his gentleman's notions make him a fine fellow, keep him from meanness and cowardice, I trust it will all turn out well. For a more loving and tender heart cannot be imagined, tho' the talents of neither of them are distinguished, which does not disappoint me, knowing well they often ruin their owners.

Kitty is only less than an Angel in looks and every qualification. Oh Dué, if you knew her and your little Beck as they are, and could [see] them every day you would say there is nothing like them. But what is truly funny is to see Beck with a little class of six or eight children, holding up her finger in silence with her pen and ink, giving them good points or crosses and keeping better order than her Mother can. Her oldest [pupil] is her own age but she is a woman to her—Kit rules books, sets copies, hears lessons, and conducts herself with such grace that girls twice her age show her the greatest respect.

And my Annina—that is the pinch—My Annina—so young, so lovely, so innocent—absorbed in all the romance of youthful passion—as I have told you, she gave her heart without my knowledge and afterwards what could a doting and unhappy Mother do but take the part of friend and confident dissembling my distress and resolving that if there was no remedy to help her, at least by my love and pity. I found her case incurable, nor do I yet know if there will be any cause for repentance as her favorite has good talents and a handsome independence. It is said, immense wealth, but I never inquired much about it—he is now on his passage to Guadeloupe to endeavor to arrange his affairs so as to settle my darling here, as she never will consent to our separation. Her poor little soul is tossed by all the hopes and fears you may imagine. He has appointed six or eight months for his return, but if it will ever be—who can tell. He has been well educated, and is possessed of good principles but there is great danger certainly.

You know I always look directly upwards. Dearest Harriet and my angel Cecil sleep in the wood [cemetery] close beside me. The children and many of our good Sisters to whom they were much attached have planted their graves with wild flowers, and the little enclosure which contains them is the dearest spot to me on earth. I do not miss them half as much as you would think, as according to my mad notions, it seems as if they are always around me, at all events separation will not be long.

My health is excellent considering [circumstances]. These good souls who call me Mother [supply me] with fresh eggs, milk and butter, coffee and cream, good vegetables, home[made] bread etc. and oblige me to live a thousand times easier and better…Never do the least kind of work of any kind, to walk around with knitting in hand and give the look of encouragement or reproof thro' the house and school is my chief business—at 5 our work finishes, and we all repair to the woods in fine weather and in wet tell woman's stories and read till supper.

So now, dearest, dear friend, I have as I would have wished you to do in my place—given you the outline—within all is quiet—no busy world, no painful whispers, no misconstructions. We are as quiet as the sheep your innocent Kit and Beck are caressing. Our chapel joins the house, the parish pastor comes every morning at six to say mass and at eight work begins…

EAS

In her new lifestyle of creative charity as foundress of the Sisters of Charity of St. Joseph's, Elizabeth was elected superior for successive terms. In this role, she was not only foundress and leader of the community, but also its animator. For individual members she was their instructor, confidant, mentor, religious formator and guide. Juggling multiple roles, in various ways, Elizabeth and many other women of her time engaged in multi-tasking long before the concept was developed or the word coined. She screened candidates, instructed novices, and counseled Sisters of Charity about the missions to which they were sent and their particular ministries.

Knowing the temperament and character of each of her companions, Mother Seton shared her wisdom with them just as she would give advices to her own children, including advice to Sister Cecilia O'Conway[4] who had first been her assistant at the school on Paca Street in Baltimore, Maryland and who became the first Sister of Charity in North America. Elizabeth wrote candidly to Sister Cecilia in order to prepare her for sharing life with companions of different temperaments and to foster spiritual stamina for the new foundation about to be made in New York.[5]

> Going on her heavenly errand...my child, often I shall say in my solitude among a 100, my Cecil is with you, my God, I find her in you. Every moment she will be serving and loving you with me—
>
> Be a *friend, Sister, comfort, and support to Rose* [White], and let Felicity [Brady][6] see that you go all on [in] Faith, and that she will find her true grace in a full confidence in Rose. Love your Mother above in her, also, my dear one.
>
> I do not feel the least uneasy about you—if you suffer, so much the better for our high journey above—the only fear I have is that you will let the old string pull too hard for solitude and silence, but look to the Kingdom of souls...My Celia—child of my Soul to OUR God, I commit you!

જાજાજાજાજા

---

[4] Cecilia Maria O'Conway was sent to establish the New York Roman Catholic Orphan Asylum in New York City in 1817.

[5] 7.107, Elizabeth Seton to Sister Cecilia O'Conway, [before August 13, 1817], *Seton Collected Writings*, 2:498.

[6] Margaret Felicita Brady (1794-1883) entered the Sisters of Charity and was known as Sister Felicity from 1814 until 1846 when she withdrew.

Postlude

Saint—Model for all Ages

Elizabeth Seton defined herself by faith not by circumstances. Her experiences span the boundaries of time and space. Today modern women and men may identify with her steadfast courage and faith-filled hope in the face of challenges, vocational discernment, and search for truth. Saint Elizabeth Ann Seton is a role model for people of all ages and walks of life as saint, mother, and foundress.

When preparing to send the first band of Sisters of Charity to her native New York in 1817, little did she know, when she referred to herself as a "citizen of the world,"[1] that over one hundred-fifty years later Pope Paul VI would add her name to the canon of saints of the Roman Catholic Church. Her life experiences as a rejected child, troubled adolescent, grief-stricken widow who parented alone were the reality which moved Elizabeth Bayley Seton from spirituality into heroic sanctity. Parents and spouses, educators and evangelizers, and anyone who wishes to risk new ventures may look to Saint Elizabeth Ann Seton for inspiration to move from what has been to what could be with the grace of God.

God used the Sulpician priests to unfold the Divine Plan for Elizabeth Seton. Reverend Simon Gabriel Bruté, S.S. (1779-1839), of Mount St. Mary's, served as Elizabeth's spiritual director until her death and was also chaplain to the Sisters of Charity until 1834. He was her principle guide on the path to sanctity. Bruté, along with DuBois, actively inculturated the spirit of Saints Vincent de Paul and Louise de Marillac within and among the Sisters of Charity.

The work of education and charity lives on around the world in Elizabeth's spiritual daughters. James Gibbons (1834-1921, later cardinal), archbishop of Baltimore, initiated her cause for canonization in 1882. Officially introduced at the Vatican in 1940, the Seton Cause made steady progress. Blessed John XXIII declared Elizabeth venerable December 18, 1959, and also prayed at her beatification March 17, 1963. Pope Paul VI canonized Saint Elizabeth Ann Seton September 14th during the Holy Year of 1975 and the International Year of the Woman. On this historic

---

[1] 7.103, Elizabeth Ann Seton to Rev. Simon Gabriel Bruté, 1 August 1817, *Seton Collected Writings,* 2:494.

occasion, Pope Paul VI remarked: "Elizabeth Ann Seton is a Saint! She is the first daughter of the United States of America to be glorified with this incomparable attribute. Rejoice for your glorious daughter."

The Holy See accepted three cures as miracles through her intercession. The beneficiaries were the following: Sister Gertrude Korzendorfer, D.C. (1872-1942), of New Orleans, from pancreatic cancer; a young child, Ann Theresa O'Neill (b.1948), of Baltimore, from acute, lymphatic leukemia; and Carl Kalin (1902-1976), of New York, from a rare form of fulminating meningo enchepalitis complicated by primary rubeola.

The Seton Legacy

The extraordinary manner in which Elizabeth lived an ordinary life flowed from the centrality of the Word of God and the Eucharist in her life. She lived her vocations fully—as wife, mother, and Sister of Charity. Encountering God in Word and Sacrament strengthened Elizabeth during life's challenges and enabled her to be a loving person toward God, her family, her neighbor, and all of creation. She undertook works of mercy and justice. Not only did she and her Sisters of Charity care for orphans, widows, and families living in poverty, but they also addressed unmet needs among persons marginalized and suffering in numerous ways. Elizabeth had a special concern for children who lacked educational opportunities, especially for religious instruction.

Her life-long response to God's will led her to sanctity. She lived out her Baptism through service to others. Her holiness developed from her early religious formation as an Episcopalian. Her trust in God and longing for Eternity began at a young age. Throughout her earthly journey of forty-six years, Elizabeth viewed herself as a pilgrim on the road of life. She faced each day with eyes of faith, looking forward to eternity.

Her life and writings are replete with her pursuit of the Divine Will, nourishment from the Eucharist and the Bible, confidence in Divine Providence, and charitable service to Jesus Christ in poor persons. From her deathbed in Emmitsburg she admonished those gathered about her: "Be children of the Church, be children of the Church."[2]

---

[2] A-7.268, Account by Rev. Simon Bruté, S.S., of Elizabeth Seton's Last Days, *Seton Collected Writings*, 2:767.

Sacred scripture framed the way Elizabeth prayed her way through life's joys and struggles. This enabled her to live serenely in the midst of uncertainty and ambiguity. Psalm 23, which she learned as a child, remained her favorite treasury of consolation throughout her life of suffering and loss. Elizabeth's pathway to inner peace and sanctity flowed from her way of living the Paschal Mystery of Jesus Christ's suffering, death, and resurrection— willing to take up and embrace the cross of Christ—and kissing it, too.[3]

Her understanding of Eucharist changed as she moved from pious reception of Holy Communion as an Episcopalian to awe as a Roman Catholic and often ecstatic adoration of the Real Presence. Her Eucharistic devotion and faith in God's abiding presence nourished her imitation of Jesus Christ, the source and model of all charity. The mission of the Sisters of Charity was one of charity and education. Elizabeth's choice of the Vincentian rule reflects how she understood their call to apostolic service as honoring Jesus Christ through service to persons in need. Elizabeth's spiritual pathway involved other people—her advisors, friends, collaborators, and those she served. The relational aspects of her spirituality were a natural gift which she used as a religious leader and animator in community.

Seton Writings. Elizabeth was a prolific writer. Extant documents are published in *Elizabeth Bayley Seton Collected Writings* (New City Press: New York). Also in her hand are some of the primitive documents of the Sisters of Charity of St. Joseph's and her own last will and testament. In addition to correspondence, Elizabeth also wrote meditations, instructions, poetry, hymns, journals, and diaries. Her journals include both spiritual reflections and chronicle accounts, like *The Italian Journal. Dear Remembrances* is an autobiographical retrospective memoir or life review. Her meditations deal with the liturgical seasons, sacraments, virtue, biblical themes, and the saints. Among her instructions are those used in preparing children for their First Communion, and conferences for the religious formation of the Sisters of Charity on such topics as service, charity, eternity, the Eucharist, and Mary, the Mother of God.

Bruté advised Elizabeth to read the lives of Saint Louise de Marillac and Saint Vincent de Paul and some of their spiritual writings. From her reading and translations of them, Elizabeth learned about the strategic importance of education for children living in poverty. As a result, she embraced education as a fundamental ministry of the Sisters of Charity.

[3] Cf. 2.7, Elizabeth Seton to Rebecca Seton, *Seton Collected Writings*, 1:257.

Elizabeth rendered the prototypical English translation of the first biographies of Louise de Marillac and Vincent de Paul: *The Life of Mademoiselle Le Gras* (Nicolas Gobillon, 1676) and *The Life of the Venerable Servant of God Vincent de Paul* (Louis Abelly, 1664). She also translated selections from the *Conferences of Vincent de Paul to Daughters of Charity* and *Notes on the Life of Sister Françoise Bony, D.C.* (1694-1759). Also among the Seton translations are excerpts from selected conferences of Saint Francis de Sales, portions of works by Saint Teresa of Avila, meditations by Rev. Louis Du Pont, S.J., and the beginning of the life of Saint Ignatius of Loyola. Elizabeth also made a translation of the eighteenth-century spiritual classic by Ambroise de Lombez, O.F.M., Cap., *A Treatise on Interior Peace.*[4]

Elizabeth had a habit of copying meaningful passages from books she was reading and of making marginal notes in her bible. Bibles containing her jottings and marginal notes are preserved in the Rare Books and Special Collections, Hesburgh Library, University of Notre Dame, Indiana, and in the Simon Bruté Collection of the Old Cathedral Library, Vincennes, Indiana. Her copybooks abound with notes from *A Commentary on the Book of Psalms* (1792) by George Horne and notes on sermons of Rev. John Henry Hobart. Elizabeth also made extracts of passages which appealed to her from the writings of George Henry Glasse on the New Testament.

Elizabeth left an enduring legacy in education for needy pupils in Catholic schools. Popular devotion acclaims Saint Elizabeth Ann Seton as a patron of Catholic schools because of her pioneer role in values-based education. Officially Saint Elizabeth Ann is patron of United States Sea Services and also of the State of Maryland.

Elizabeth's journey of faith presents an outstanding model for all people because her vision of faith remains relevant today. In a letter to her lifelong friend Julia Sitgreaves Scott, Elizabeth summarized her way of life: "Faith lifts the staggering soul on one side, hope supports it on the other, experience says it must be and love says let it be."[5] Saint Elizabeth Ann Seton died in the White House near Emmitsburg, January 4, 1821, surrounded by her Sisters of Charity and daughter Catherine Josephine. Her remains repose there in the Basilica of the National Shrine of Saint Elizabeth Ann Seton, Emmitsburg, Maryland. See www.setonshrine.org.

[4] Ambroise de Lombez, *A Treatise on Interior Peace*, ed. by Marie Celeste Cuzzolina, S.C., (Staten Island, NY: Alba House, 1996).
[5] 6.30, Elizabeth Seton to Julia Scott, *Seton Collected Writings*, 2:117.

The Sisters of Charity of St. Joseph's grew and blossomed into several independent communities in North America: The Sisters of Charity of Saint Vincent de Paul of New York (1846); the Sisters of Charity of Cincinnati (1852); the Sisters of Charity of Saint Vincent de Paul of Halifax (1856); the Sisters of Charity of Saint Elizabeth, Convent Station, New Jersey (1859); and the Sisters of Charity of Seton Hill, Greensburg, Pennsylvania (1870). As a result of mandates from their General Assembly (1829 and 1845) requiring the Sulpicians to return to their founding charism of the education and formation of priests, the Sulpician superiors arranged for the Emmitsburg-based Sisters of Charity of St. Joseph's to join (1850) the Daughters of Charity of Saint Vincent de Paul of Paris, France. These six communities formed the *Conference of Mother Seton's Daughters* (1947) which developed into *The Sisters of Charity Federation* (2006) with member congregations from the United States and Canada. Federation members are rooted in the tradition of Vincent de Paul and Louise de Marillac.

Saint Elizabeth Ann Seton was a person of faith, rooted in the Word of God and nourished by the Eucharist. Like Miriam of Nazareth who became the Mother of Jesus, Elizabeth pondered her feelings about life events in prayer.[6] She shared her reflections in her correspondence with loved ones in the family and among dear friends. Grounded in the realities of circumstances and commitments, Elizabeth's letters reveal her life of faith and the friendships of her soul. Elizabeth Ann Seton became a saint to whom we look today as a realistic model for contemporary Christian living.

- Faith-filled commitment to God in Spirit and Truth
- Fidelity to her vocation in life
- Steadfast courage in the face of adversity
- Biblical and Eucharistic spirituality
- Creative charity in pursuit of mission

Her wisdom and example reveal God's action in her daily life and in her circle of family and friends. Through all events and relationships, Elizabeth sought God alone, desiring to do the will of the Father just as Jesus did. Her message for us today is the same as in her generation:

---

[6] Luke 2:19.

And what was the first rule of our dear Saviour's life? You know it was to do his Father's will. Well, then, the first end I propose in our daily work is to do the will of God; secondly, to do it in the manner he wills it; and thirdly, to do it because it is his will.[7]

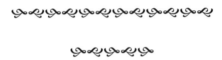

[7] Charles Ignatius White, *The Life of Mrs. Eliza Seton* (E. Dunigan and Brother: New York, 1853), 340.

Appendix A
Chronology
Saint Elizabeth Ann Seton (1774-1821)
Mother—Foundress—Saint

28 August 1774

Born in or near New York City as Elizabeth Ann Bayley.

25 January 1794

Married William Magee Seton (1768-1803).

3 May 1795

Gave birth to a daughter, Anna Maria Seton, who died 12 March 1812, and was buried in Saint Joseph's Cemetery, Emmitsburg, MD.

25 November 1796

Gave birth to a son, William M. Seton, who died 13 January 1868, and was buried in Mount St. Mary's Cemetery, Emmitsburg, MD.

January 1798

Business failure and financial problems loomed on the horizon, culminating with the death on 9 June of her father-in-law, William Seton, senior, and the deterioration of her husband's health from tuberculosis.

20 July 1798

Gave birth to a son, Richard Bayley Seton, who died 26 June 1823, on board the *Oswego* and was buried at sea off the coast of Liberia.

28 June 1800

Gave birth to a daughter, Catherine Charlton Seton, who died 3 April 1891, and was buried in Sisters of Mercy Calvary Cemetery, Woodside, NY.

7 December 1800

Officials made inventory of family assets in conjunction with bankruptcy proceedings.

20 August 1802

Gave birth to a daughter, Rebecca Mary Seton, who died 3 November 1816 and was buried in Saint Joseph's Cemetery, Emmitsburg, MD.

2 October 1803

Departed New York with William Magee Seton and daughter Anna Maria to sail for Italy on the *Shepherdess*.

18 November 1803

Arrived at the port of Livorno where the Setons were immediately quarantined in the San Jacopo Lazaretto because officials feared yellow fever (then spreading in New York).

19 December 1803

Released from quarantine and moved into a rented apartment in Pisa.

27 December 1803

William Magee Seton died in Pisa and was buried the next day in the English cemetery at Livorno. His remains were transferred and reinterred in the Sta. E. A. Seton Parish garden of Livorno in 2004.

8 April 1804

The Widow Seton and Annina sailed for New York in the company of Antonio Filicchi on the *Pyomingo*.

4 June 1804

The Setons and Antonio Filicchi arrived at the port of New York.

14 March 1805

Made profession of faith in the Roman Catholic Church at Saint Peter's, Barclay Street, NY.

25 March 1805

Received first Holy Communion as a Roman Catholic at Saint Peter's, Barclay Street, NY.

25 May 1806

Received the sacrament of Confirmation from Bishop John Carroll at Saint Peter's, Barclay Street, NY.

9 June 1808

Mrs. Seton and her daughters sailed from New York for Baltimore, MD, on the *Grand Sachem*.

15 June 1808

The *Grand Sachem* arrived in the port of Baltimore at Fell's Point but the Setons did not disembark until the next morning.

16 June 1808

The Setons arrived at Saint Mary's Seminary as the new Chapel of the Presentation was being dedicated. Soon Mrs. Seton began a school for girls on Paca Street in Baltimore, MD.

29 June 1808

Traveled to Washington, D.C., in the company of Rev. Michael Hurley, O.S.A., and seminarian, Samuel Sutherland Cooper, in order to bring her sons, William and Richard, to Baltimore, MD, for enrollment at Saint Mary's College.

7 December 1808

Cecilia Maria O'Conway arrived from Philadelphia, PA, and became the first candidate for the Sisters of Charity.

25 March 1809

Mrs. Seton pronounced private vows of chastity and obedience for one year before Bishop Carroll who bestowed on her the title of Mother Seton.

9 June 1809

Mother Seton and companions dressed alike in the black dress, cape, and cap as Sisters of Charity on the Feast of Corpus Christi.

21 June 1809

Mother Seton and the first group left Baltimore for Emmitsburg, MD.

22 June 1809

The first group of travelers arrived at Emmitsburg but had to take up temporary residence at Mount St. Mary's because their stone farm house in the Valley was not yet repaired. Rev. John Dubois gave them hospitality in a cabin called "Mr. Duhamel's house."

29 July 1809
Elizabeth Seton welcomed the second group, from Baltimore to Saint Joseph's Valley. The travelers included Rose White, two boarders, Isabella O'Conway and Julia LeBreton, along with Sisters Cecilia O'Conway, Mary Ann Butler, Susan Clossey, and Kitty Mullan.

30 July 1809
Mother Seton and companions attended Sunday mass at Saint Joseph's Church in the village of Emmitsburg, MD.

31 July 1809
Founded the Sisters of Charity of Saint Joseph's and began community life, according to a provisional rule, in the Stone House at Saint Joseph's Valley near Emmitsburg, MD.

23 December 1809
Death of Henrietta (Harriet) Seton, sister-in-law of Elizabeth, the first to die in Saint Joseph's Valley and to be buried in the original graveyard, Saint Joseph's Cemetery, on the property of the Sisters of Charity.

22 February 1810
The Sisters of Charity opened Saint Joseph's Free School, the first free Catholic school for girls staffed by religious women in the United States.

17 April 1810
Death of Cecilia Seton, sister-in-law of Elizabeth, who was buried in St. Joseph's Cemetery, Emmitsburg, MD.

14 May 1810
Establishment of Saint Joseph's Academy, a tuition-based school for girls.

22 August 1810
Rev. Benedict Flaget, S.S., left Baltimore for Emmitsburg, MD, with a French copy of the *Common Rules of the Daughters of Charity* for the Sulpicians to translate and adapt for use by the Sisters of Charity of St. Joseph's.

17 January 1812
Official confirmation of the *Regulations of the Sisters of Charity in the United States* based on the *Common Rules of the Daughters of Charity* by Vincent de Paul and Louise de Marillac, founded in 1633.

12 March 1812
Death of Annina, first vowed member of the Sisters of Charity of St. Joseph's, and eldest child of Elizabeth Seton.

19 July 1813
First vow group of eighteen sisters pronounced vows for the first time under the American version of the Daughters of Charity rule.

29 September 1814
Elizabeth Seton sent Sister Rose Landry White, Sister Susan Clossey, and Sister Teresa Conroy to Philadelphia, PA, to staff Saint Joseph's Asylum, the community's first mission beyond Emmitsburg, MD, and the first Catholic orphanage in the United States.

12 July 1815
Mother Seton established a mission of the Sisters of Charity at Mount St. Mary's, near Emmitsburg, MD, in order to staff the infirmary, support liturgical ministries, and direct domestic services.

3 November 1816
Death of Rebecca, youngest child of Elizabeth Seton.

27 January 1817
The Senate of the Maryland General Assembly gave final approval for the legal incorporation of the Sisters of Charity of St. Joseph's in the State of Maryland.

28 August 1817
Mother Seton sent Sisters Rose White, Cecilia O'Conway, and Felicitas Brady to begin the New York Roman Catholic Orphan Asylum in New York City.

4 January 1821

Mother Seton died in the White House, Emmitsburg, MD.

22 August 1882

After celebrating mass at Elizabeth Seton's tomb, James Cardinal Gibbons proposed the possibility of her canonization.

30 October 1907

Informative Cause of Process for Canonization began, which concluded by forwarding Elizabeth Seton's writings to Rome in 1925.

5 January 1935

Cure of Sister Gertrude Korzendorfer, D.C. (1872-1942) in New Orleans, from cancer of the pancreas.

15 January 1936

Decree by the Sacred Congregation of Rites that "no obstacle exists against taking further steps relative to the Cause."

28 February 1940

Pope Pius XII signed the Decree of Introduction of the Cause for Beatification and Canonization of the Servant of God, Elizabeth Ann Bayley, the Widow Seton.

28-29 October 1947

Establishment of the Conference of Mother Seton's Daughters which developed into the collaborative association, Sisters of Charity Federation.

13 April 1952

Cure of Ann Theresa O'Neill (b. 1948) from leukemia in Baltimore, MD.

18 December 1959

Blessed John XXIII proclaimed the Heroicity of Virtues of Elizabeth Bayley Seton and declared her Venerable Mother Seton.

9 October 1963

Cure of Carl Kalin (1902-1976) of New York from fulminating meningo enchepalitis complicated by primary rubeola.

17 March 1963

The beatification of Blessed Elizabeth Ann Seton occurred during the pontificate of Blessed John XXIII.

18 April 1963

The relics of Blessed Elizabeth Ann Seton were enshrined over the main altar of Saint Joseph College, Emmitsburg, MD.

4 January 1968

The relics of Blessed Elizabeth Ann Seton were transferred to the new chapel of the Daughters of Charity, Emmitsburg, MD, which is now designated as the Shrine of Saint Elizabeth Ann Seton. The Seton reliquary was enshrined beneath the altar of Saint Elizabeth Ann Seton in the chapel dedicated to her memory.

14 September 1975

Pope Paul VI canonized Saint Elizabeth Ann Seton who became the first native-born person of the United States to be declared a saint in the Roman Catholic Church.

13 February 1991

Designation of the Chapel of Saint Elizabeth Ann Seton as a minor basilica. The public celebration for the bestowal of this honor on the Basilica of the National Shrine of Saint Elizabeth Ann Seton was August 4 in Emmitsburg, MD.

4 January

Feast day of Saint Elizabeth Ann Seton, who was a pioneer in free Catholic education and popularly considered a patron of Catholic schools in the United States. Officially Saint Elizabeth Ann Seton is patron of United States Sea Services and also of the State of Maryland.

Appendix B

Seton Sites of Interest

Italy

Livorno (Leghorn) in Tuscany

Parrocchia Sta. Elisabetta Anna Seton (Parrochia Madre Seton), Piazza G. M. Lavagna, 16, Livorno, Italy, 57125. (www.madreseton.it)

United States of America

Maryland

The Mother Seton House at *Saint Mary's Spiritual Center and Historic Site* on Paca Street, 600 N. Paca Street, Baltimore, MD 21201 (www.stmarysspiritualcenter.org)

The National Shrine of Saint Elizabeth Ann Seton, 333 South Seton Avenue, Emmitsburg, MD 21727 (www.setonshrine.org)

New York

Saint Andrew's Episcopal Church, 4 Arthur Kill Road, Richmond Town, Staten Island, NY 10306-1197 (www.churchofstandrew-si.com)

Saint Paul's Episcopal Chapel, 209 Broadway, between Vesey and Fulton Streets, New York, NY 10007 (www.saintpaulschapel.org)

Saint Peter's Catholic Church, 16 Barclay and Church Streets, New York, NY 10007 (www.archny.org)

Shrine of Saint Elizabeth Ann Seton, Church of Our Lady of the Rosary, 7 State Street, New York, NY 10004 (www.setonshrine.com)

Trinity Episcopal Church, 74 Trinity Place on Broadway at Wall Street, New York, NY 10006 (www.trinitywallstreet.org)

Appendix C

Recommended Reading

Alderman, Margaret, and Josephine Burns, D.C. *Praying with Elizabeth Seton.* Winona, WI: Saint Mary's, 1992. Print. Companions on the Journey Series.

Bechtle, S.C., Regina, and Margaret Egan, S.C., eds. *All Creation Sings.* New York: Sisters of Charity of New York, 2009. Print.

Bechtle, S.C., Regina, Judith Metz, S.C., eds., and Ellin M. Kelly, mss. ed. *Elizabeth Bayley Seton Collected Writings.* 3 Vols. New York: New City, 2000-2006. Print.

Dirvin, C.M., Joseph I. *The Soul of Elizabeth Seton A Spiritual Portrait.* San Francisco, CA: Ignatius, 1990. Print.

Elizabeth Seton: Bridging Centuries Bridging Cultures. Papers from *The Seton Legacy Symposia of 1996-1997.* Vincentian Studies Institute of the United States: *Vincentian Heritage.,* 18, no. 2 (1998). Print.

Elizabeth Seton in Dialogue with Her Time and Ours. Papers from *The Seton Legacy Symposium of 1992.* Vincentian Studies Institute of the United States: *Vincentian Heritage,* 14, no. 3 (1993). Print.

Kelly, Ellin M., Ed., *Elizabeth Seton's Two Bibles. Her Notes and Markings.* Huntington, Indiana: Our Sunday Visitor, 1977. Print.

Kelly, Ellin M. *Numerous Choirs. A Chronicle of Elizabeth Bayley Seton and Her Spiritual Daughters. The Seton Years, 1774-1821.* Vol. 1. Evansville, IN: Daughters of Charity, 1981. Print.

Laverty, S.C., Rose Maria. *Loom of Many Threads. The English and French Influences on the Character of Elizabeth Ann Bayley Seton.* New York: Paulist Press, 1958. Print.

McNeil, D.C., Betty Ann. *15 Days of Prayer with Elizabeth Seton.* Liguori, MI: Liguori Publications, 2003. Print.

McNeil, D.C., Betty Ann. *Light & Grace. Elizabeth Ann Seton on Life, Faith, and Eternity.* Emmitsburg, MD: Sisters of Charity of St. Joseph's, 2009. Print.

Melville, Annabelle, and Ellin M. Kelly. *Elizabeth Seton Selected Writings.* New York: Paulist, 1987. Print.

Melville, Annabelle M. *Elizabeth Bayley Seton 1774-1821.* Ed. Betty Ann McNeil, D.C., Hanover, PA: The Sheridan Press, 2009. Print.

Metz, S.C., Judith. *Judith Metz, S.C., A Retreat with Elizabeth Seton. Meeting our Grace.* Cincinnati, OH: Saint Anthony Messenger, 1999. Print.

About the Editor

Sister Betty Ann McNeil, a native of Virginia Beach, Virginia, entered the Daughters of Charity at Emmitsburg, Maryland, in 1964. She earned a master of social work from Virginia Commonwealth University (1975) and has worked as a clinical social worker in a variety of institutional, parish, and community based settings. She has represented the Emmitsburg Province of the Daughters of Charity on the Vincentian Studies Institute of the United States since 1988 and currently serves on the Editorial Board of *Vincentian Heritage* for the Vincentian Studies Institute of DePaul University, Chicago, Illinois. Sister Betty Ann serves as Provincial Archivist for the Daughters of Charity, Province of Emmitsburg, Maryland.

Sister Betty Ann served on the Advisory Committee for the publication of the multi-volume opus *Elizabeth Bayley Seton Collected Writings* (New City Press). Her publications include, *The Vincentian Family Tree*, a monograph. She is a contributor to the *New Catholic Encyclopedia* (2002) and has had articles published in *Review for Religious*, *The Vincentian Heritage*, and *Vincentiana*.

Her most recent publications include the following: co-author with Martha Libster Ph.D., R.N., C.N.S., of *"Enlightened Charity: The Holistic Nursing Care, Education, and Advices Concerning the Sick of Sister Matilda Coskery, D.C. (1799–1870),"* (Golden Apple Publications, 2009); author of *Light & Grace, Elizabeth Ann Seton on Life, Faith, and Eternity* (Emmitsburg: 2009); and editor of the revised edition of the definitive biography by Annabelle Melville, *Elizabeth Bayley Seton 1774-1821* (Hanover: 2009).

In *Friendship of My Soul,* Sister Betty Ann has not only compiled and edited the Seton material presented on family, faith, and friendship but has authored the introduction for each section, the conclusion and postlude. In addition, she has organized valuable information in appendixes for readers to pursue further study or visit significant sites related to Saint Elizabeth Ann Seton.